新时代高等院校大学英语系列教材
大学通识教育课程系列

总主编 俞洪亮

主编 田美
副主编 杨瑞英
编者 田美 彭凤玲 杨瑞英
陈大地 韩璐 葛冬梅

中国大学MOOC『中西文化比较』课程配套教材

中西文化比较（第3版）

Chinese and Western Cultures:
A Comparative Perspective (The 3rd Edition)

西安交通大学出版社
XI'AN JIAOTONG UNIVERSITY PRESS

图书在版编目（CIP）数据

中西文化比较：英文 / 田美主编. -- 3版.
西安：西安交通大学出版社，2024.6. -- ISBN 978-7-5693-3858-4
Ⅰ.G04
中国国家版本馆CIP数据核字第20241K6U05号

中西文化比较（第3版）
Chinese and Western Cultures: A Comparative Perspective (The 3rd Edition)

总 主 编	俞洪亮
主 编	田 美
责任编辑	蔡乐芊
责任校对	许方怿
装帧设计	伍 胜

出版发行	西安交通大学出版社 （西安市兴庆南路1号 邮政编码710048）
网　　址	http://www.xjtupress.com
电　　话	（029）82668357 82667874（市场营销中心） （029）82668315（总编办）
传　　真	（029）82668280
印　　刷	陕西日报印务有限公司
开　　本	850mm×1168mm 1/16 印张 13 字数 300千字
版次印次	2016年4月第1版 2021年4月第2版 2024年6月第3版第1次印刷
书　　号	ISBN 978-7-5693-3858-4
定　　价	54.80元

如发现印装质量问题，请与本社市场营销中心联系调换。
订购热线：（029）82665248　（029）82667874
投稿热线：（029）82665371
版权所有　侵权必究

总 序

当今世界正处在百年未有之大变局，以新能源、新材料、大数据、人工智能等为代表的新一轮科技革命加速演进，中国制造2025、教育现代化2035等国家重大战略布局，对高等教育发展，尤其是人才培养和人才供给产生了深刻的影响，也提出了全新的命题。我们要把准新一轮科技革命和产业革命的新脉搏，坚持以社会需求为导向，深入推进本科专业布局调整和教育教学改革，让一流本科教育真正满足新时代对一流本科人才的需求。

世界现代大学发展史表明，本科教育是高等教育的立命之本、发展之本。回归本科教育已经成为世界一流大学共同的行动纲领。党和国家加快推动本科教育振兴，持续推进本科人才培养模式改革，从"四新建设"到"双万计划"，从构建高校思政工作体系到全面实施课程思政……推进一流本科教育的步伐行稳致远、张弛有度。2019年9月，教育部印发《关于深化本科教育教学改革全面提高人才培养质量的意见》，同年12月，教育部印发《普通高等学校教材管理办法》，对立德树人的人才培养根本任务、课程建设质量的全面提高和高水平教材的编写及使用等方面提出了意见。

发展外语教育是全球的共识，外语教育伴随国家发展阶段的变化而变化。进入新时代，外语教育的使命与责任更加重大，高等外语教育的发展关系到高等教育人才的培养质量。在中国新一轮的高等教育改革中，大学英语教育教学要立足新的发展阶段，主动服务国家战略需求，主动融入新文科建设，适应高等教育普及化阶段的需求和特点，拥抱新未来和新技术，在建设更高质量的课程中获取改革与发展的新动能，在融合发展中开辟大学英语课程建设的新路径。

教材关乎国家事权，是铸魂工程，是构建高质量高等教育体系的重要内容，也是课堂教学的重要载体和实现人才培养的有力保障。因此，推进新时代教材建设，必须体现马克思主义中国化要求，体现中国和中华民族风格，体现党和国家对教育的基本要求，体现国家和民族基本价值观，体现人类文化知识积累和创新成果。2021年是中国共产党成立100周年和"十四五"规划开局之年，也是开启全面建设社会主义现代化强国新征程的第一年，我们在这个重要历史节点上，以全面贯彻党的教育方针，落实立德树人根本任务为宗旨，紧扣国家对推进新文科建设的需求，并以《大学英语教学指南（2020版）》为指导，组织编写了这套"新时代高等院校大学英语系列"教材，力求培养心系祖国发展、积极参与全球竞争、思维方式创新、融贯中西文化的新时代人才。

本系列教材分为两个子系列，分别为"大学通识教育课程系列"和"专门用途英语系列"，以知识、能力、素养和价值为本位，体现通识教育与专业教育的有机结合。具体来讲，本系列教材的特色如下：

1. 思政统领，落实立德树人的根本任务，坚持价值和能力双重导向

"新时代高等院校大学英语系列"教材全面贯彻党的教育方针，落实立德树人根本任务，扎根中国大地，站稳中国立场，充分体现社会主义核心价值观，强化爱国主义、集体主义、社会主义教育，展现中华优秀传统文化，将构建人类命运共同体、"一带一路"倡议、中国制造2025等热点话题有机融入在教材编写中，使学生在真实场景中习得知识，提升能力，引导学生坚定道路自信、理论自信、制度自信、文化自信，增强学生"讲好中国故事"的底气和能力。

2. 聚焦一流建设，融入"双万计划"，发挥示范引领作用

本系列教材遵循高起点、高标准、高要求的原则，融入一流专业和一流课程建设，对标金课"两性一度"，从体系搭建、内容架构、问题设置等方面打造全方位、多维度的示范性教材，反映学科发展的最新进展，引入高等外语教育改革最新成果，写好教材这个"人才培养的主要剧本"。

3. 融入"四新"建设，体现学科交叉融合，服务创新人才体系

大学英语教育在新工科、新医科、新农科和新文科建设中被赋予了新的责任和使命。面对新一轮的科技浪潮和全球变局，大学英语教育成为创新型、复合型、应用型、国际化人才培养体系的重要一环，也是服务跨学科创新人才培养不可或缺的基础。本系列教材中不仅有对人工智能、大数据和区块链发展等新兴交叉学科的探讨，也有对医学、艺术、教育、科技、农业等传统领域的拓展。这些教材能够帮助不同学科背景的学生拓宽视野，培养创新思维，增强思辨能力。

4. 落实"学生中心"育人理念，尊重个体差异，实现教学资源多样化

智能教育时代学生的思维特点、学习习惯和现代信息技术的持续发展都对教材的内容和形态提出了新的要求。学生学习的方式和获取资源的渠道日趋多样化，教材也要走好线上线下融合的道路。同时，教师的教育观、教学观、教材观、学生观、质量观等均发生了变化。多形态的教材建设和数字化学习资源供给成为新一轮大学英语建设的重要内容。本系列教材配套慕课、示范微课、在线练习、音频和视频等各类知识服务资源，产生"教"与"学"的互动，提升学生的参与感、获得感和成就感。

5. 面向中西部高校，推动优质教育均衡发展，满足学生更高水平的需求

高等教育的整体质量是我国构建高质量教育体系的重要标志。本系列教材加强东部与西部高校间协同合作，观照中西部地区高等院校目标读者，增加展现中西部地区人文特色，以及社会和科技发展成果的最新内容，依据中西部高校的教学实际编写，适应国家和区域经济社会发展需求。

"新时代高等院校大学英语系列"教材编写团队成员均是具有丰富教学经验、专业知识背景和先进教学理念的骨干教师，来自西安交通大学、兰州大学、西北工业大学、西安电子科技大学、扬州大学、西北师范大学、宁夏大学、河南科技大学、西安外国语大学、西北政法大学等多所院校。

一流人才培养须"知行合一"。我们组织编写的这套具有中西部特色，体现东部与西部合作的高水平、高质量、高起点的"新时代高等院校大学英语系列"教材正是对国家人才培养战略部署的积极响应，希望它如同一艘航船，带领老师和同学们驶向更广阔的海洋。

List of figures

Figure 1.1	The levels of culture and their interaction
Figure 1.2	Pictures on Chinese and Western cultural differences
Figure 5.1	The Indo-European language family
Figure 5.2	Major branches of Tibeto-Burman
Figure 5.3	Illustration of the difference in writing system
Figure 6.1	Reflective practice example 1
Figure 6.2	Reflective practice example 2
Figure 7.1	*Peonies* by Giuseppe Castiglione (1688–1766)
Figure 7.2	*Peony "Dancing Black Lion"* by Zou Yigui (1688–1772)
Figure 7.3	*Madame Monet in kimono* by Claude Monet (1840–1926) in 1876
Figure 7.4	*Almond Flowers* by Vincent van Gogh (1853–1890)
Figure 7.5	Cave paintings at Lascaux
Figure 7.6	Painting from Mount Helan
Figure 7.7	The Venus of Willendorf
Figure 7.8	Goddess of Hongshan
Figure 7.9	The "Mask of Agamemnon"
Figure 7.10	Houmuwu square cauldron (后母戊鼎)
Figure 7.11	Arch of Constantine
Figure 7.12	Terracotta Army
Figure 7.13	Series of ancient Roman portrait sculptures
Figure 7.14	*Horse Treads on a Hun* (马踏匈奴)
Figure 7.15	*Mosaic of Theodora and Retinue*
Figure 7.16	*Ladies with Head-pinned Flowers* (《簪花仕女图》) by Zhou Fang (周昉)
Figure 7.17	*Snow Mountains* by Guo Xi
Figure 7.18	*Mona Lisa* by Leonardo da Vinci (1452–1519)
Figure 7.19	*Court Ladies of the Former Shu* (《王蜀宫妓图》) by Tang Yin (唐寅)
Figure 7.20	Manifestations of culture at different levels
Figure 7.21	*View of Delft* by Johannes Vermeer
Figure 7.22	*Landscapes of the Four Seasons* by Shi Tao
Figure 7.23	Cultural product design model
Figure 8.1	Structures of Petrarchan and Shakespearean sonnets

Figure 8.2   Development of sonnet rhyming schemes in England
Figure 8.3   The portrait of Shakespeare
Figure 8.4   The cover and head pages of *Shakespeare's Sonnets*, published in 1609
Figure 8.5   Elizabeth Barrett Browning (1806–1861)
Figure 8.6   Portrait of Su Shi (1037–1101)
Figure 8.7   *Huan Wo He Shan* by Yue Fei (1103–1142)
Figure 8.8   Feng Zhi (1905–1993)
Figure 8.9   Ezra Pound (1885–1972)
Figure 8.10 *After Wei Wang's Snow over Rivers and Mountains* by Wang Shimin (1592–1680)
Figure 8.11 Alfred, Lord Tennyson (1809–1892)
Figure 8.12 The song *Guan Ju* of *the Classic of Poetry*
Figure 8.13 Robert Frost (1874–1963)
Figure 8.14 William Wordsworth (1770–1850)

List of tables

Table 4.1	Power distance index (PDI)
Table 4.2	Individualism (IDV) index
Table 4.3	Long-term orientation (LTO) index
Table 4.4	Images of the cultural *Other*
Table 5.1	Differences in word forms between the two texts
Table 5.2	Comparison of a word formation method in Chinese and English

Contents

0 Introduction: Understanding Globalization, Belt and Road Initiative, and Intercultural Competence in an Evolving World　/ 1

　　0.1　Globalization　/ 2

　　0.2　Belt and Road Initiative　/ 4

　　0.3　Impact of the Belt and Road Initiative: Significance of Developing Intercultural Competence　/ 5

　　0.4　Structure of the Book　/ 9

　　0.5　Case Study Assignment　/ 11

1　Understanding Culture　/ 14

　　1.1　Culture: The Definitions　/ 14

　　1.2　Characteristics of Culture　/ 16

　　1.3　Classification of Culture　/ 18

　　1.4　Culture, Race and Ethnicity　/ 20

　　1.5　Comparative Analysis of Cultures: The Methodology　/ 21

　　1.6　Understanding Culture: More Appropriate Attitudes　/ 26

　　1.7　Chapter Summary　/ 27

　　1.8　Case Study Assignment　/ 27

2　Comparing Origins of Civilizations　/ 30

　　2.1　Origins of Chinese and Western Civilizations　/ 31

　　2.2　Differences Between Chinese and Western Civilizations　/ 34

　　2.3　Origin and Development of Civilizations　/ 45

　　2.4　Chapter Summary　/ 46

　　2.5　Case Study Assignments　/ 46

3 Comparing Chinese and Western Philosophy　/ 50
　　3.1　Knowing Chinese and Western Philosophy　/ 52
　　3.2　Comparing the View of the World　/ 58
　　3.3　Comparing View of Knowledge and Truth　/ 62
　　3.4　Chapter Summary　/ 66
　　3.5　Case Study Assignments　/ 67

4 Comparing Values　/ 71
　　4.1　Definitions of Values　/ 71
　　4.2　Reflective Observation　/ 72
　　4.3　Abstract Conceptualization: Stereotyping and Stereotypes　/ 78
　　4.4　Active Experimentation: Re-thinking Hofstede's Value Dimensions　/ 79
　　4.5　Common Values of Humanity　/ 80
　　4.6　Chapter Summary　/ 82
　　4.7　Case Study Assignment　/ 82

5 Languages and Thinking Patterns　/ 85
　　5.1　A Brief Definition of Language　/ 86
　　5.2　Language and Language Families　/ 87
　　5.3　Differences between English and Chinese　/ 90
　　5.4　Thinking and Thinking Patterns　/ 98
　　5.5　The Relationship Between Language and Thought　/ 101
　　5.6　Chapter Summary　/ 102
　　5.7　Case Study Assignments　/ 103

6 Perspectives on Education: A Comparative Approach　/ 106
　　6.1　Abstract Conceptualization　/ 109
　　6.2　Concrete experience　/ 110
　　6.3　Reflective observation and comparison　/ 111
　　6.4　Case Study Assignment　/ 117
　　6.5　Chapter Summary　/ 118

7 Comparing Cultures Through Visual Arts / 121
    7.1 Concrete Experience / 121
    7.2 Reflective Observation / 125
    7.3 Abstract Conceptualization / 139
    7.4 Active Experimentation / 145
    7.5 Chapter Summary / 151
    7.6 Case Study Assignment / 152

8 Comparing Cultures Through Poetry / 157
    8.1 Concrete Experience / 157
    8.2 Reflective Observation / 159
    8.3 Abstract Conceptualization / 177
    8.4 Active Experimentation / 187
    8.5 Chapter Summary / 189
    8.6 Case Study Assignment / 191

0

Introduction: Understanding Globalization, Belt and Road Initiative, and Intercultural Competence in an Evolving World

Tian Mei

Globalization is a term we often hear, and it profoundly influences our everyday lives, shaping the world as we know it. This introductory chapter begins with an interpretation of globalization from scholars such as David Harvey and Anthony Giddens. They guide our understandings of how modern technology and communication have revolutionized our perceptions of time and space. We then explore globalization's role in today's business strategies and its significant impact on social and cultural interactions worldwide. Yet, the chapter emphasizes that globalization is a double-edged sword; while it is praised for connecting diverse worlds, it has also faced criticism for obscuring cultural diversity.

Against this backdrop, China's Belt and Road Initiative proposes a more inclusive and collaborative approach to globalization. Rooted in the ancient Silk Road's heritage, this initiative seeks economic cooperation while promoting a world where diverse traditions enrich one another. Within the Belt and Road Initiative's framework, the significance of intercultural competence becomes apparent. This competence encompasses the knowledge, skills, and attitudes necessary for effective intercultural communication and cooperation. As our world grows more interdependent, the ability to navigate and embrace cultural diversity is vital, illuminating the relevance and necessity of this book.

0.1 Globalization

0.1.1 What Globalization is

Globalization reshapes our world, compressing time and space in ways that were previously unimaginable, as described by scholars such as David Harvey and Anthony Giddens. Specifically, Harvey (1989, p.240) defined globalization as a form of *"time-space compression"*, highlighting how advancements in technology and communication have dramatically changed our perception of time and space, effectively shrinking the world. Similarly, Giddens (1994) views globalization as a transformative influence on space and time, intensified by the advent of instantaneous global communication and mass transportation.

A further review of the research literature reveals three primary perspectives on globalization: as a historical process, a business strategy, and a force of social and cultural interaction. Historically, globalization is not a recent phenomenon; rather, global connections have been present for millennia. For example, Samovar et al. (2012) refer to the Silk Road as an early example of globalization, where the transport of goods from China through Central Asia to the Roman Empire from 1200 to 700 BCE marked an initial phase of global trade and cultural exchange, while Marco Polo's travels along this route in the late 13th century emphasize the long-standing nature of global interaction.

From a business viewpoint, globalization is seen as *"the spread of products, technology, information, and jobs across nations"* (Fernando et al., 2024). The International Monetary Fund (IMF, 2008) echoes this view, describing globalization as *"the increasing integration of economies around the world"*. IMF further illustrates how globalization has manifested in different aspects of the global economy: the increase in trade value, foreign direct investment, international financial claims, and labor mobility—all evidence of growing global economic interdependence.

Finally, globalization acts as a driving force for social and cultural interaction. Globalization has accelerated social, political, and economic changes at an unprecedented pace. This process enhances global interconnectedness in all facets of social life, from cultural practices to financial systems, and even spiritual dimensions (Held et al., 1999).

0.1.2 How globalization impacts our daily lives

Globalization's impact on our daily lives can be vividly illustrated through the operations of multinational corporations like Apple, KFC, and Starbucks. For example, Apple's well-known products, such as iPhones, iPads, and MacBooks, are designed in Silicon Valley, but produced by Chinese manufacturers. Another example is KFC, one of the first Western fast-food chains to enter China. In January 1999, Starbucks opened its first store in Beijing. By 2023, there were 6,804 Starbucks stores in China (statista.com, 2024), which introduced and popularized coffee culture in our traditional tea-drinking society. In the same year, the Chinese Luckin Coffee reached 10,829 stores in China, surpassing Starbucks as the largest coffee chain brand in China (Chiang, 2024). Luckin Coffee has adapted the traditional coffee menu to local tastes, offering Moutai-flavored coffee, showing how globalization can lead to a fusion of different cultures.

The increasing number of internationally mobile students further evidences the impact of globalization on social and cultural interaction. In 1975 there were roughly 0.6 million students pursuing higher education outside of their home country. The number increased to 5.6 million in 2018 (Organisation for Economic Co-operation and Development [OECD], 2020). Although international student mobility was negatively affected by COVID-19, the pandemic also demonstrated how online teaching and learning could shift the potential for international exchange. One example is an online course on Chinese culture provided by the authors of this book, which hosted over eight hundred international students from more than ten countries in summer 2023 (Xjtu.edu.cn, 2023). As the United Nations Educational, Scientific and Cultural Organization (UNESCO) has predicted, *"...the future of student mobility will combine physical international experiences with digitally driven virtual opportunities that reach a wider range of students..."* (p.41).

It is worth noting that globalization is not seen merely as a neutral process of cultural interaction. Rather, it has been widely criticized for leading to cultural homogenization, a process where diverse traditions are assimilated into a monolithic framework dominated by Western influences (Tomlinson, 1999). In other words, Western-dominated global exchanges are not reciprocal but rather a dissemination of Western, particularly American, norms and values (Friedman, 1999), which erodes the richness of global cultural diversity.

0.2 Belt and Road Initiative

0.2.1 A brief introduction to the Belt and Road Initiative

The Belt and Road Initiative was launched by China in 2013. It comprises two components: the "Silk Road Economic Belt" and "the 21st-century Maritime Silk Road." The former establishes land connections linking China with Southeast Asia, South Asia, Central Asia, Russia, and Europe. The latter develops maritime routes extending from China to Southeast and South Asia, the South Pacific, the Middle East, Eastern Africa, and Europe. These routes serve not just as conduits for goods, but also for fostering cooperation and cultural exchanges, embodying the initiative's goal to *"enhance the network and cooperation between countries, to establish comprehensive, multi-leveled, and integrated networks of connectivity, and to achieve diversified, independent, balanced and sustainable development in countries along its pathway"* (Yidaiyilu.gov.cn, 2023).

The Belt and Road Initiative places high priority on policy coordination, facility connectivity, unimpeded cross-border commerce, and financial integration (United Nations, 2022). At its core is the concept of connectivity, involving not only policies and businesses but also cultures. Its emphasis on people-to-people bonds highlights the significance of cultural and educational exchanges in deepening mutual understanding and trust among different nations. Reflecting this ethos, President Xi Jinping has stressed the value of cultural exchanges, referencing Zhang Qian's diplomatic missions to Central Asia in the Han Dynasty as a *"chapter of friendship that has been passed down through the ages"* (People.cn, 2013).

The Belt and Road Initiative stands as China's most important initiative on international cooperation, contributing to the building of *"a community of shared future for mankind"*. Through this initiative, China calls for international collaborative efforts to achieve common development and prosperity and to establish a community with shared interests and responsibilities that transcends political, economic, and cultural divides, emphasizing *"mutual political trust, economic integration, and cultural inclusiveness"* (State Council Information Office, 2023).

0.2.2 Comparing the Belt and Road Initiative with Western-led globalization

Following Albrow (2018), we now summarize the differences between Western-led globalization with China's Belt and Road Initiative, considering historical, economic, and cultural perspectives. Historically, Western-led globalization is often seen as the dissemination of Western modernity and industrialization, emphasizing a world order led by Western ideals. In contrast, the Belt and Road Initiative draws on the 2,000-year history of the Silk Road, highlighting a longstanding tradition of cultural exchanges and stressing continuity in international cooperation throughout human history.

Economically, the distinction is apparent as Western globalization is driven by multinational companies pursuing global expansion and profit maximization, whereas the Belt and Road Initiative takes a different approach. This initiative seeks to mobilize economic resources alongside scholarly efforts to achieve global prosperity and well-being. Culturally, while Western globalization faces criticism for leading to cultural homogenization, often equated with Americanization, the Belt and Road Initiative prioritizes cultural understanding, communication, and cooperation, presenting a more inclusive form of globalization that respects cultural diversity and promotes mutual learning and exchange.

In sum, the Belt and Road Initiative proposes an alternative model of globalization, one that not only acknowledges but embraces cultural plurality. It links to the building of a community of shared future for mankind, aspiring to create *"an open, inclusive, clean and beautiful world"* where different cultures can coexist and benefit from each other's strengths.

0.3 Impact of the Belt and Road Initiative: Significance of Developing Intercultural Competence

0.3.1 What intercultural competence is

Intercultural competence has been defined by many scholars, among whom Michael Byram, Darla Deardorff, and Milton Bennett are most influential. Specifically, Byram (1997) in his Multidimensional Model of Intercultural Competence suggests that intercultural competence comprises three core components: knowledge, skills, and attitudes. Knowledge refers to an understanding of *"social groups and their products and practices in one's own and in one's interlocutor's country, and of the general processes of societal and individual interaction"* (p.51). Skills include those of interpreting and relating and those of discovering and interacting. The skills of interpreting and relating refer to the ability to *"interpret a document or event from another culture, to explain it, and relate it to documents from one's own"* (p.52). The skills of discovering and interacting refer to the ability to *"acquire new knowledge of a culture and cultural practices and the ability to operate knowledge, attitudes, and skills under the constraints of real-time communication and interaction"* (p.52). Attitudes involve curiosity and openness, and *"a readiness to suspend disbelief about other cultures and belief about one's own"* (p.50). For Byram, the combination of knowledge, skills, and attitudes lay the ground for building interpersonal and intercultural relationships on the basis of mutual respect and understanding.

Deardorff's (2006) Process Model of Intercultural Competence emphasizes the reflective nature of intercultural learning and the ongoing adaptation that underpins intercultural competence. The model begins with knowledge, comprehension, and skills, which lead to desired internal outcomes such as adaptability, flexibility, an ethnorelative view, and empathy. These personal attributes facilitate effective communication in intercultural situations, which further leads to the formation of appropriate attitudes, including respect for others from different cultural backgrounds, openness, and curiosity.

A further conceptual model of intercultural competence is Bennett's (2004) Developmental Model of Intercultural Sensitivity. The theory conceptualizes how individuals perceive and respond to cultural differences in a progression of six stages, developing from ethnocentrism to ethnorelativism. The model begins with *denial*, where one's understanding of cultural difference is limited, and advances to *defense*, where a dichotomous categorization of "us-versus-them" is common. *Minimization* follows, where the assumed similarities between us and others are based on one's own cultural worldviews, thus still holding one's own culture central.

As intercultural sensitivity develops, one moves to *acceptance*, *recognizing* and *appreciating* cultural differences. At acceptance, individuals become conscious that the cultures of self and others are equally complex but different in form. Adaptation allows one to empathize with and enact appropriate behaviors in different cultures. Integration enables a person to move flexibly among cultures, encouraging the formation of a third-culture identity.

0.3.2 Why intercultural competence is important

The development of intercultural competence is crucial, particularly within the context of the Belt and Road Initiative. Economic factors highlight the demand for individuals with intercultural competence. As of August 2023, 1.15 million overseas companies have established operations in China (RegistrationChina.com, 2023). In 2021 foreign direct investment in China grew by 14.9%, reaching a record high of 1.15 trillion yuan (Xinhuanet.com). The success of these companies is heavily reliant on the support of the local workforce. Meanwhile, the Belt and Road Initiative has catalyzed Chinese companies' expansion overseas. For instance, news reports indicated that in 2023, 854 new Chinese firms set up branches in Uzbekistan, 210% more than in 2022, making China the leading country for new businesses there (Interfax.com, 2024). These Chinese enterprises abroad require their employees to be competent in managing daily routine business operations within diverse cultural settings.

In addition, in today's world, individuals from varied cultural backgrounds have become an integral part of our everyday lives—our neighbors, teachers, friends, and colleagues—making the development of intercultural competence imperative for college students to effectively engage with the increasing diversity in our society. In fact, the lack of intercultural competence can hinder intercultural communication, reduce the willingness to communicate interculturally, and potentially lead to intercultural misunderstanding or conflict.

0.3.3 How the book helps to develop intercultural competence

Earlier in this section (0.3.1), we have introduced Byram's (1997) Multidimensional Model of Intercultural Competence, Deardorff's (2006) Process Model of Intercultural Competence, and Bennett's (2004) Developmental Model of Intercultural Sensitivity. When we compare these models, a common theme emerges: effective intercultural communication involves not just acquiring knowledge but also requires the development of specific skills and the cultivation of appropriate attitudes towards cultural differences. Otten (2003) reinforces this interpretation by stressing that intercultural competence involves a long-term cognitive transformation, as represented by an increase in one's cultural knowledge, emotional transformation, as represented by attitude changes, and behavioral transformation, in terms of gaining intercultural skills. This comprehensive development enables meaningful and positive interactions with members of different cultures, highlighting the multifaceted nature of intercultural competence.

Based on these three models, *Chinese and Western Cultures: A Comparative Approach* (3rd Edition) helps college students to develop intercultural competence in the areas of knowledge, skills, and attitudes. Regarding knowledge, the book includes chapters on the history of civilization, traditional philosophy, cultural values, languages, literature, and arts. We emphasize the importance of understanding both *"knowledge of our own culture and that of others"* by comparing Western and Chinese cultures (Byram, 1997, p.51).

In addition, this book assists students in developing English language skills, as we believe that linguistic competence is crucial for culturally appropriate behavior (Gregersen-Hermans, 2020). Following Byram (1995), we also encourage students to develop skills in discovering, exploring, and interpreting cultural phenomena, as well as in applying intercultural theories to their daily life experiences.

More importantly, this book helps students to develop appropriate attitudes to facilitate intercultural communication. Specifically, it aims to increase students' awareness of problematic attitudes in intercultural communication, such as stereotypes, bias, prejudice, racism, ethnocentrism, culturalism, and Eurocentrism:

> **Cultural stereotypes** are oversimplified, over-generalized, and often inaccurate beliefs about the traits of members of different groups.
>
> **Bias** and **prejudice** involve deeply held negative feelings towards a specific group, are often rooted in stereotypes, and can result in discrimination.
>
> **Racism** is an extreme form of prejudice, where individuals or groups are discriminated against based on their race.
>
> **Ethnocentrism** refers to the belief in the inherent superiority of one's own ethnic group or culture over others'.
>
> **Culturalism** arises from the tendency to impose static and uniform cultural traits on diverse societies, thus overlooking the complexities of cultural change.

> **Eurocentrism** is an ideology that often positions Western civilization at the center of cultural narratives, casting it as the standard against which all other cultures are judged. Within this framework, "the East" is frequently depicted with negative or exotic attributes, serving to reinforce a positive and unchallenged image of "the West" (Holliday, 2005).

Furthermore, this book helps to cultivate the following attitudes in intercultural communication. Specifically, adopting a mindset of curiosity and sensitivity towards cultural diversity promotes understanding and connection (see also Kedia & Mukherji, 1999). Striving for a broader perspective encourages an appreciation for differences and recognition of each culture's unique contributions. Balancing uncertainty, tensions, and chaos demonstrates adaptability, which is crucial for navigating diverse cultural contexts. Managing change and committing to lifelong learning are integral for sustained success in intercultural interactions. These attitudes establish a foundation for harmonious exchanges of ideas across cultural boundaries.

0.4 Structure of the Book

Building a community with a shared future for mankind and promoting international cooperation based on the Belt and Road Initiative demand interculturally competent college graduates. *Chinese and Western Cultures: A Comparative Approach* (3rd Edition), aligning with such demand, helps to develop college students' intercultural competence. This book introduces Chinese and Western cultures from an intercultural perspective. Drawing upon teaching and research contributions from multiple disciplines, it discusses a variety of cultural and intercultural topics. Activities and case study assignments are designed, encouraging students to reflect on the increasing complexity of global issues and supporting the development of intercultural awareness and intercultural competence in the real world.

This book consists of eight chapters, apart from this introduction. Chapters One to Three lay a foundation for the discussion. Chapter One by Tian Mei introduces the definitions, key features and categorization of culture. By discussing the problems of ethnocentric and essentialist views of culture, Chapter One proposes a dialectical approach to intercultural analysis. Chapter Two by Peng Fengling outlines a brief history of Chinese and Western civilizations. It also discusses the influences of geographical and socio-economic environments on the early stages of development in Chinese and Western civilizations. Chapter Three, also by Peng Fengling, briefly discusses Chinese and Western philosophy from the perspectives of the view of the world, view of values, and view of knowledge and truth.

The following parallel chapters compare different aspects of Chinese and Western cultures, i.e. cultural values, language and thinking patterns, educational practices, visual arts, and poetry. Chapter Four by Tian Mei reviews commonly believed Chinese and Western values, pinpointing the problems of over-simplified and over-generalized descriptions as represented by Hofstede's value dimensions. This chapter then introduces the common values of all mankind, a concept stressing the significance of respecting diverse cultures and acknowledging the openness and exchanges of cultures.

Chapter Five by Yang Ruiying focuses on the comparison of languages and the modes of thinking. It starts with a definition of language and language families and then compares English and Chinese languages at the sound, words and sentence levels. In light of the differences in the respective languages belonging to different language families, it compares the modes of thinking of Western and Chinese people and briefly discusses the relationship between language and thought.

Chapter Six by Carla Briffett-Aktaş reviews the literature on Western and Chinese educational differences. A variety of perspectives are discussed and students are encouraged to reflect on the purposes of education, how teaching, learning, and assessment are conducted in different regions, and the educational commonalities that exist between Western and Chinese contexts.

Chapter Seven, written by Chen Dadi, Han Lu, and Ge Dongmei, focuses on the development of Chinese and Western art and aesthetics. Drawing on the cultural level model, the chapter examines the interaction between culture and art, emphasizing the role of art in intercultural communication. It also introduces Dutton's (2009) core features of art, facilitating students' comprehension of the shared elements between Chinese and Western arts.

Moving forward, Chapter Eight, authored by Chen Dadi and Ge Dongmei, reviews the cultural influences on classical Chinese *Ci* and English sonnets. This chapter further explores the aesthetic dimensions of poetry, encompassing its sound, sight, and "soul". Through thought-provoking discussions, this last chapter encourages students to promote Chinese poetry in intercultural communication.

This book was originally written for undergraduate students taking *Chinese and Western Cultures: A Comparative Approach*, a general education core course at Xi'an Jiaotong University. It can be used as a book in cultural study courses and intercultural communication courses. Lecturers may find the concepts, theories, activities, and case study assignments useful as training materials for workshops. In addition, the book may be of value to the readers who are interested in Chinese and Western cultures and would like to improve English proficiency through cultural studies.

In a speech given at the College of Europe in Belgium, President Xi Jinping expressed his hope for the youth to break down the barriers of stereotypes, bias, and racism, approaching the world with "*equality, respect, and love*". We would like to conclude this introductory chapter with this quote:

> 希望中欧双方的同学们用平等、尊重、爱心来看待这个世界，用欣赏、包容、互鉴的态度来看待世界上的不同文明，促进中国和欧洲人民的相互了解和理解，促进中国、欧洲同世界其他国家人民的相互了解和理解，用青春的活力和青春的奋斗，让我们生活的这个星球变得更加美好。(I hope that Chinese and European students will perceive the world with equality, respect, and love, and treat different civilizations with appreciation, inclusiveness and a spirit of mutual learning. In doing so, we can promote mutual understanding and knowledge among the people of China, Europe, and other parts of the world. With your youthful energy and hard work, you can make our planet a better place to live in.)

0.5 Case Study Assignment

Please write a 300-word essay explaining your understanding of and reflection on the following material. Your essay should be well-argued, well organized, and clearly written, and should contain few grammar, syntax, or spelling errors.

> 这个世界，各国相互联系、相互依存的程度空前加深，人类生活在同一个地球村里，生活在历史和现实交汇的同一个时空里，越来越成为你中有我、我中有你的命运共同体。
>
> （2013年3月23日，习近平在莫斯科国际关系学院的演讲）

References

Albrow, M. (2018). *China's role in a shared human future towards theory for global leadership*. New Star Press.

Bennett, M. J. (2004). Becoming interculturally competent. In J. S. Wurzel (Ed.), *Toward multiculturalism: A reader in multicultural education* (pp. 62–77). Intercultural Resource Corporation.

Byram, M. (1997). *Teaching and assessing intercultural communicative competence*. Multilingual Matters.

Chiang, S. (2024). How Luckin coffee overtook Starbucks as the largest coffee chain in China. https://www.cnbc.com/2023/09/12/how-luckin-coffee-overtook-starbucks-in-china.html#:~:text=Luckin%20Coffee%20grew%20to%2010%2C829%20stores%20in%20China,following%20what%20one%20analyst%20calls%20an%20%E2%80%9Caggressive%E2%80%9D%20expansion

Deardorff, D. (2006). The identification and assessment of intercultural competence as a student outcome of internationalization at institutions of higher education in the United States. *Journal of Studies in International Education*, 10(3): 241–266. https://doi.org/10.1177/1028315306287002

Fernando, J., Anderson, S., & Rubin, D. (2024). Globalization in business with history and pros and cons. https://www.investopedia.com/terms/g/globalization.asp

Friedman, T. (1999). *The Lexus and the olive tree: Understanding globalization*. Picador.

Giddens, A. (1994). *Beyond left and right*. Stanford University Press.

Gregersen-Hermans, J. (2020). *Intercultural competence development in higher education*. Routledge.

Harvey, D. (1989). *Condition of post-modernity*. Blackwell.

Holliday, A. (2005). *The struggle to teach English as an international language*. Oxford University Press.

interfax.com (2024). China leads by number of businesses opened in Uzbekistan in 2023. https://interfax.com/newsroom/top-stories/98447/

International Monetary Fund (2008). Globalization: A brief review. https://www.imf.org/external/np/exr/ib/2008/pdf/053008.pdf

Kedia, B. L., & Mukherji, A. (1999). Global managers: Developing a mindset for global competitiveness. *Journal of World Business*, 34(3): 230–251. https://doi.org/10.1016/s1090-9516(99)00017-6

Organisation for Economic Co-operation and Development (2020). What is the profile of internationally mobile students. https://www.oecd-ilibrary.org/education/education-at-a-glance-2020_974729f4-en#:~:text=International%20student%20mobility%20has%20been%20expanding%20quite%20consistently,study%2C%20more%20than%20twice%20the%20number%20in%202005

Otten, M. (2003). Intercultural learning and diversity in higher education. *Journal of Studies in International Education*, 7(1): 12–26. https://doi.org/10.1177/1028315302250177

People.cn (2013). Xi Jinping: People of the countries along the silk road have jointly written a friendly chapter that has been passed down through the ages. http://politics.people.com.cn/n/2013/0907/c1024-22840805.html

RegistrationChina.com (2023). How many foreign companies in China. https://www.registrationchina.com/articles/how-many-foreign-companies-in-china/#:~:text=By%20the%20end%20of%20August%202023%2C%20a%20total,data%20provided%20by%20the%20Ministry%20of%20Commerce%20%28MOFCOM%29

Samovar, L., Porter, R., & McDaniel, E. (2012). *Cross-cultural communication* (7th ed.). Peking University Press.

State Council Information Office, China (2023). The Belt and Road Initiative: A key pillar of the global Community of Shared Future. http://www.scio.gov.cn/zfbps/zfbps_2279/202310/t20231010_773734.html

Statista.com (2024). Number of Starbucks stores in China. https://www.statista.com/statistics/277795/number-of-starbucks-stores-in-china/#:~:text=China%20had%20the%20most%20Starbucks%20stores%20in%20Asia,than%205%2C000%20Starbucks%20stores%20in%20operation%20in%20China

Tomlinson, J. (1999). *Globalization and culture*. University of Chicago Press.

Xinhuanet.com (2022). China's FDI inflow up 14.9 pct to record high in 2021. https://english.news.cn/20220113/54ad6a22de304803b0d890ca48a7f4a7/c.html

Xjtu.edu.cn (2023). 2023 XJTU linking-the-world summer school course "A Glimpse of Chinese Culture from a Comparative Perspective" were successfully held. https://news.xjtu.edu.cn/info/1219/199878.htm

Yidaiyilu.gov.cn (2023). What is the BRI? https://eng.yidaiyilu.gov.cn/p/0N4P7CF0.html.

United Nations (2022). Partnering for a brighter shared future. https://eng.yidaiyilu.gov.cn/wcm.files/upload/CMSydylyw/202209/202209190500015.pdf

United Nations Educational, Scientific and Cultural Organization (2022). Moving minds: Opportunities and challenges for virtual student mobility in a post-pandemic world. https://www.iesalc.unesco.org/wp-content/uploads/2022/03/IESALC_220315_RE_VSM_EN.pdf

1
Understanding Culture

Tian Mei

Culture is a concept closely relevant to our lives. Culture is significant because it distinguishes human beings from lower animals, and all humans live in cultures which in turn influence our ways of thinking and behaving. Culture is an umbrella term covering almost all social phenomena, from education to religion, from language to modes of behavior, from thinking patterns to value systems, from arts and literature to economic and political activities. Commonly used as it is, culture is difficult to define. It has different meanings for researchers in different areas. Given the significance of culture to human life, this chapter is devoted to an exploration of the meaning of the concept.

This chapter will first introduce the definitions, characteristics and classification of cultures. It will then focus on differences between the concept of culture and two other terms, i.e. race and ethnicity. The subsequent section of the chapter analyzes problematic attitudes in intercultural communication. A dialectical methodology will be proposed as a more appropriate approach in intercultural studies.

1.1 Culture: The Definitions

Activity 1-1 Please write down whatever comes to your mind when you hear or think of "culture". "Iceberg" and "fish in water" are metaphors that people have used to refer to culture. What do the metaphors tell you? Try and give your own definition of culture.

Culture is a term difficult to define. Williams (1983) once noted that culture is one of the two or three most complicated words in the English language. Kroeber & Kluckhohn in 1952 in their book *Culture: A Critical Review of Concepts and Definitions* identified 164 different meanings of the term from British and American sources alone. In our book, we will not provide a singular definition of culture, as this would be restrictive rather than thought-provoking. Following Martin & Nakayama (2009), we propose that it is more appropriate to interpret the concept from different perspectives so as to embrace its complexity.

Social science researchers view culture as the totality of cultural values, beliefs, and norms, which guides our perceptions and behaviors. For example, an introductory book on sociology defines *"culture"* as *"the language, beliefs, values and norms, customs, roles, knowledge, and skills which combine to make up the way of life of any society"* (Browne, 2011, p.10). Similarly, Matsumoto (1996, p.16) describes culture as " ... *the set of attitudes, values, beliefs, and behaviors shared by a group of people, but different for each individual, communicated from one generation to the next*".

In the field of anthropology, researchers put emphasis on culture as communicative patterns. Verbal and nonverbal activities bear significance for these researchers when defining culture, who believe that through communicative activities, social members acquire social knowledge. Geertz (1973, p.89), a representative anthropologist, defines culture as:

> ... a historically transmitted pattern of meaning embodied in symbols, a system of inherited conceptions expressed in symbolic forms by means of which men communicate, perpetuate and develop their knowledge about and attitudes towards life.

In recent years, many scholars have tended to study culture from a critical perspective. Critical theoretical perspective perceives culture as contingent, dynamic and ever-changing, while social actions and personal identities are restricted by regulationws, social rules and "power of discourse". The following quote, for example, suggests that:

> ... definitions of culture as "shared and transmitted from generation to generation"... in a linear and seemingly static fashion ... [may] suppress and erase marginalized voices and experiences.
>
> (Yep, as cited in Collier et al., 2002, p.231)

1.2 Characteristics of Culture

Activity 1-2   The previous section reviews the ways that culture has been defined by sociologists. Different as the definitions are, they tend to stress similar features. Below are another three representative definitions. Read these definitions and summarize the characteristics of culture that they draw attention to.

> Culture consists of patterns, explicit and implicit, of and for behavior acquired and transmitted by symbols, constituting the distinctive achievements of human groups, including their embodiment in artifacts; the essential core of culture consists of traditional (i.e. historically derived and selected) ideas and especially their attached values.
> (Kroeber & Kluckhohn, 1952, p.181, as cited in Spencer-Oatey, 2009)

> [Culture is] … the set of attitudes, values, beliefs, and behaviors shared by a group of people, but different for each individual, communicated from one generation to the next.
> (Matsumoto 1996, p.16, as cited in Spencer-Oatey, 2009)

> Culture is a fuzzy set of basic assumptions and values, orientations to life, beliefs, policies, procedures and behavioral conventions that are shared by a group of people, and that influence (but do not determine) each members' behavior and his/her interpretations of the "meaning" of other people's behavior.
> (Spencer-Oatey 2000, p.4, as cited in Spencer-Oatey, 2009)

As reflected in the above definitions, culture has the following major characteristics. To study "culture", it is crucial for us to be aware of these characteristics:

1.2.1 Culture is learned

Culture is not an innate instinct of human beings. It is not like looking, sleeping, or sneezing that one was naturally able to do once one was born. Instead, it is about behaviors that we learn by interacting with others (e.g. how to speak appropriately to fit social and physical contexts in which speaking takes place).

Starting from early childhood, human beings learn how to behave in socially and culturally acceptable ways. Children growing up and being socialized in different cultures may learn to react differently to similar social stimuli in similar situations. For example, a Chinese child growing up in Chinese culture is more likely to learn to eat with chopsticks while a British kid growing up in British culture is more likely to learn to eat with knife and folk.

1.2.2 Culture is shared

Culture cannot be possessed by any single individual. It is something created, practiced and shared by a cultural group. Literary works, painting, architecture, tradition, beliefs, and values are all shared by people of a culture. As Ferraro (1998, p.16) once stated:

> There is, in other words, no such thing as the culture of a hermit. If a solitary individual thinks and behaves in a certain way, that thought or action is idiosyncratic, not cultural. For an idea, a thing, or a behavior to be considered cultural, it must be shared by some type of social group or society.

1.2.3 Culture is transmissive

Culture can be transmitted from one generation to the other. Language, which takes the forms of writing, speaking, listening, and reading, plays a vital role in this process. Via language, the current generation is able to inherit cultural achievements accumulated in the earlier generations, to add in new values, or to replace old values with new ones and to pass on the "whole" set of cultural traits to the next generation. The transmission process assures the continuation and consistency of culture through human history. It should be noted that this process can also involve cultural changes that occur and are transmitted.

1.2.4 Culture affects human behavior

Culture provides a set of rules and norms that influence people's thinking and behaving. That is to say, culture guides activities conducted by human beings based on their interpretation of what would be culturally appropriate. Hofstede (1991, p.8) once pointed out *"cultural meaning ... lies precisely and only in the way these practices are interpreted by the insiders [of a given culture]"*. These "invisible" values affect our perceptions, which in turn affect our behaviors.

1.3 Classification of Culture

Culture is manifested in different layers of depth. Therefore, it can be classified in different ways.

1.3.1 Visible and invisible culture

To analyze the culture of a social group, we need to distinguish two types of cultural artifacts, i.e. visible artifacts and invisible ones. Many researchers have classified cultural elements based on whether these elements can be felt, touched and observed. A well-known example is Triandis et al.'s (1980) classification. According to this classification, physical culture refers to objects, such as roads, buildings, and tools. Subjective culture refers to a wide range of topics, such as communication patterns, family roles, values and social systems.

Similarly, Schein (1984, p.4, see Figure 1.1) divides cultural artifacts into three groups, i.e. artifacts and creations, values and basic assumptions.

Figure 1.1
The levels of culture and their interaction

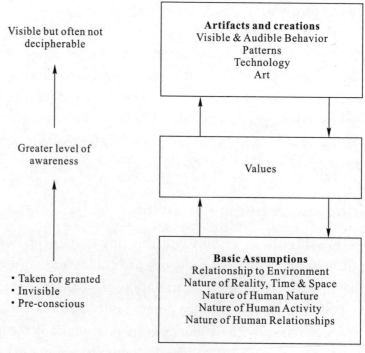

(Schein, 1984, p.4)

Artifacts and creations include visible and audible behavior, patterns, technology and art. Values are rules that govern people's behavior but cannot be directly observed. The significance of Schein's classification is that it further divides values into two types. One is debatable, for which "value" applies, while the other is non-debatable and usually taken for granted, known as basic assumptions. Unexamined assumptions can be dangerous as they may turn human behavior into unconscious and uncritical processes.

1.3.2 High and low culture

Gans (1999) divides cultural elements into two groups, i.e. high culture and popular culture. High culture includes intellectual, literary and artistic works and the activities producing it, such as education, literature, geography, art, and concerts. Popular culture includes cultural products produced to cater for the interests of the masses. Films, pop music, television dramas, magazines, and newspapers are all forms of popular culture.

Such a categorization, as reflected from the name, often correlates with social class differences. High culture is associated with the richer and more powerful social groups because education and formal training, which usually involve financial payment, are required to appreciate higher cultural products, such as literature, opera, and arts. By contrast, special training is usually not necessary to enjoy popular culture.

Activity 1-3   Do you agree that certain cultural forms are more advanced than others? Please present evidence to support your stance.

1.3.3 Mainstream and subculture

In sociology and anthropology, the terms "mainstream/dominant culture" and "subculture" are often used to refer to the cultural elements shared by different social groups within a society. Komarovsky & Sargent (1949, p.143) define subcultures as *"cultural variants displayed by certain segments of the population ... they are within the larger world of our national culture"*. In other words, when a group in a modern society shares a culture, which contains not only elements of the mainstream/dominant culture but also some features that are characteristic of this group, the group culture is known as a subculture.

Modern societies tend to have many sub-cultures: The more dynamic and socially diversified the society is, the more subcultures it has. Subculture is primarily applied to groups segmented by class, race, ethnicity, age and gender. There are, for example, youth culture and Chinese American culture. The excerpt below is extracted from Hofstede (1991, p.10). It exemplifies the different categories, i.e. "different levels of cultures". According to Hofstede (1991), a person can be influenced at the same time by a national culture, a regional or ethnic or religious or linguistic culture, a gender culture, and a generation culture. There are also subcultures associated with a person's social roles, social class, occupation and profession.

> ... a national level according to one's country (or countries for people who migrated during their lifetime); a regional and/or ethnic and/or religious and/or linguistic affiliation, as most nations are composed of culturally different regions and/or ethnic and/or religious and/or language groups; a gender level, according to whether a person was born as a girl or as a boy; a generation level, which separates grandparents from parents from children; a role category, e.g. parent, son/daughter, teacher, student; a social class level, associated with educational opportunities and with a person's occupation or profession; for those who are employed, an organizational or corporate level according to the way employees have been socialized by their work organization.
>
> (Hofstede, 1991, p.10)

1.4 Culture, Race and Ethnicity

Culture, race and ethnicity are often used interchangeably in research and everyday life. Related as they are, these three terms are different.

Activity 1-4 Imagine you are applying for a summer school course in an English-speaking country. On the application form, you are asked to choose from a list of options (such as Asian, Chinese, American Indian, Black, Latino, and White) under a certain category. What is the category likely to be named: race, culture or ethnicity?

A race is usually defined as a population which shares unique genetic and biological features that distinguish it from other groups. The term stresses physical characteristics which a person was born with, such as skin color, hair color, and facial features. Rather than a neutral medical or biological term, race has strong social and political implications. To categorize people, usually those of color, by their race is arbitrary. It fails to recognize that over 99% of the genetic features (i.e. DNA) in human beings are common to all people—that is, human beings have much more that is common than that is different. Besides, it over-emphasizes physical differences among groups and fails to recognize the complexity of each individual within the group. It is one of the major causes of failure in intercultural communication. An example of it in history is apartheid in South Africa when the rights of the black inhabitants were seriously oppressed.

Ethnicity refers to a group of people who share a culture, e.g. a history, tradition, and language. The relationship between ethnicity and culture, however, is not straightforward. For example, many second- and third-generation of Chinese people in the United Kingdom recognize themselves as ethnically Chinese and call themselves Chinese British. The culture of these second- or third-generation immigrants tends to be a hybrid of a historical culture of origin and the culture of the host country.

To distinguish culture from race and ethnicity is of significance. The interchangeable uses of these three terms are usually problematic because it makes us unable to tell the inappropriateness of the so-claimed differences among cultural groups. As Holliday (2004, p.21) observed:

> Culture is a concept which needs to be handled carefully. Nowadays it is much used, often far too loosely. One of the problems is that the most common use of the word ... conjures up vague notions about nations, races and sometimes whole continents, which are too generalized to be useful.

1.5 Comparative Analysis of Cultures: The Methodology

1.5.1 Cultural differences and cultural similarities

Human beings share certain biological and emotional features. We all need to eat, drink and sleep; thus, we need to work to secure enough food and a place to stay. We all have the ability to feel sad, happy, depressed, hurt, afraid, anxious, worried, and proud; and thus, we need language to share our emotions with each other. Our needs and desires are, on the one hand, our limitations, which create troubles and bring about difficulties. On the other hand, they open up possibilities. We have to cooperate to solve all those problems; communication and cooperation result in the formation and continuous development of human cultures.

Since all cultures are constructed by human beings, and all human beings share some similar qualities, certain elements can be found in all cultures. For example, in primitive societies, humans had to hunt for food, teach children the skills for survival, choose leaders and follow orders within a group. In modern societies, every culture has an education system, political and economic structures, and a value system. For this reason, all cultures are overlapping.

However, the specific forms that a society's educational, economic, and political systems can be different. The same applies to values, beliefs, and social norms. In other words, despite similar needs to satisfy our desires, the specific cultural artifacts that people develop, cultural practices we conduct and value systems regulating such conducts are various. For example, many Western people tend to have a cold breakfast while the majority of the Chinese prefer hot meals. In this sense, cultures are different.

1.5.2 Comparing individuals' behaviors: Differences and similarities

Activity 1-5　You are the only Chinese among some English-speaking Americans. One of them is telling a joke. All of a sudden, everyone is laughing, but you don't know why, even if you have no difficulty in understanding each word of the joke. You then decide you will no longer hang out with them because you feel you cannot understand them and you are so culturally different. How would you interpret the above case?

On the one hand, the case tells us that connotation of words can be a key to understanding. People from different cultures are likely to misunderstand each other because they are not socialized in similar social contexts and usually do not share a specific language, traditions, perceptions, values, and beliefs. In other words, culture is a complex tool through which people interact with other social members. As discussed in 1.2.4, culture affects how we perceive and how we behave.

Besides, culture not only facilitates communication between people but also creates a feeling of belonging and togetherness among people in society.

It gives us an identity of who we are. For this reason, when people migrate and settle in another country, they tend to go through a period when they feel stressed and less secure.

Moreover, the case tells us how easily we would intentionally or non-intentionally create the absolute differences between "*us*" and cultural "*others*". When we are trying to define our culture, in our mind, we have firstly depicted what other cultures are like. That is to say, culture is not what we perceive as who we are, but what we perceive as distinguishing us from each other as members of a social group. It focuses not only on what is shared with some but also on what makes us different from others.

1.5.3 Comparing cultures: Some problematic tendencies

Activity 1-6 Read the following extracts taken from Avruch (1998, pp.14-16) on culture and cultural differences. Why does the author believe such understandings are inappropriate?

> 1. Culture is homogeneous. This presumes that a (local) culture is free of internal paradoxes and contradictions such that (a) it provides clear and unambiguous behavioral "instructions" to individuals—a program for how to act—or (b) once grasped or learned by an outsider, it can be characterized in relatively straightforward ways ("the Dobuans are paranoid"). A homogeneous view of culture makes the second inadequate idea easier to sustain, namely that:
>
> 2. Culture is a thing. The reification of culture—regarding culture as a thing—leads to a notion that "it" is a thing that can act, almost independently of human actors. There is no hint of individual agency here ... The term is used as a shorthand way of referring, as we shall see, to bundles of complicated cognitive and perceptual processes, and it is a series of short (cognitive) steps from shorthand to metonymy to reification. But we should be on guard, particularly since by reifying culture it is easy to overlook intracultural diversity, underwriting the third inadequate idea:
>
> 3. Culture is uniformly distributed among members of a group. This idea imputes cognitive, affective, and behavioral uniformity to all members of the group. Intracultural variation, whether at the individual or group level, is ignored or dismissed as "deviance". Connected to this is the further misconception that:

> 4. An individual possesses but a single culture ... In fact, as we will argue, for any individual, culture always comes in the plural. A person possesses and controls several cultures in the same way, as sociolinguists tell us, that even a so-called monolingual speaker controls different "registers" of the same language or dialect.
>
> ...
>
> 5. Culture is timeless ... the idea that culture is timeless imputes a changeless quality to culture, especially to so-called traditional ones.
>
> These five inadequate ideas about culture are related and mutually reinforcing. Using them, we argue, greatly diminishes the utility of the culture concept as an analytical tool for understanding social action, in this case, conflict and conflict resolution.
>
> (Avruch, 1998, pp.14-16)

In the following, the problematic attitudes in intercultural communication, known as ethnocentrism and essentialism, will be discussed. The more appropriate attitudes in intercultural studies will then be presented.

Ethnocentrism and cultural relativism

Ethnocentrism is a cultural attitude, which holds that one's own culture is better than others'. Here we need to distinguish two concepts, ethnic identity and ethnocentrism. As has been discussed earlier, members in an ethnic group are likely to share a language, values, norms, beliefs and customs. Such cultural features—some cultural changes too—have been passed on from one generation to the next. They help to define a person and give him/her a sense of belonging. They play an important role in identifying a group and distinguishing it from other "different" groups. They contribute to group solidarity and loyalty. Ethnic diversity is one characteristic of modern multicultural society. It provides rich opportunities for inter-ethnic communication, and hence, contributes to intercultural understandings.

Ethnocentrism, however, is different. It describes a tendency that members of an ethnic group believe their own culture is not only different from other cultures but, rather, superior to others'. It is called "-centrism" because one's own ethnic culture is regarded as the center that all other cultures should learn from and should be judged from. Ethnocentrism is in nature prejudice, bias, and discrimination. It usually leads to intercultural misunderstandings, often causes failures of intercultural communication, and can result in intercultural conflicts. We all tend to hold ethnocentric perceptions, consciously or unconsciously, to evaluate, and de-value, other cultures. Once we believe our ways of behaving and thinking are the only correct ways, we are making the mistake of ethnocentrism. An example of ethnocentric perceptions is that when exposed to another culture, either as tourists or overseas students, we feel the other culture is odd, strange, and foreign. Rather than critically reflecting on our culture, we become self-defensive, judging and criticizing the other culture.

A different attitude to approaching cross-cultural differences is cultural relativism. Cultural relativism is the opposite of ethnocentrism. It is the recognition that all cultures are equal, and no culture is holding a superior position to others. Researchers advocating cultural relativism acknowledge cultural differences. They believe that different social and cultural groups are likely to have different values, conduct different cultural practices, and follow different social rules. They argue that such differences cannot be used to judge the relative excellence of the cultures; that is, whether the culture in discussion is better and more civilized than other cultures.

Cultural relativism, therefore, is about understanding cultures on their own terms. It warns us to avoid the tendency to judge various cultures via a single set of standards. The critical questions that cultural studies seek to answer, according to cultural relativism, is not whether a culture is good or not, but how the culture is formed and maintained and why people in that culture behave in a certain way. Cultural relativism encourages us to observe, analyze, and compare cultures objectively, so as to understand and appreciate cultures.

Essentialism and anti-essentialism

Buciek (2003, p.9) defines strong essentialism as a belief that *"things and phenomena have a real, true core or essence, a consistency and a determined ability which defines what the phenomenon is"*. It is a notion that a person's experiences can be described in a stable and fixed way. It assumes a member of any group would have experiences which are unchangeable through time, space, or different social contexts.

As discussed in Section 1.3.3, there are various ways to categorize people and all these categories are mingled with each other (Hofstede, 1991, p.10); that is, everybody has multiple identities, and those identities are changeable.

A strong essentialist position, however, views those categories/identities in a separable way, with a focus only or primarily on one way of categorization (e.g. a cultural belief), rather than on the basis of possible categorizations (e.g. gender, class, race, ethnicity), which are interconnected with each other. For example, people holding a strong essentialist position may expect that female students from an upper-class white British family would have the same experiences in school as a male student from a working-class African American family simply because these students are learning in a Western culture.

Anti-essentialism is an opposite epistemological approach. It encourages us to embrace the full complexity of individual experiences. Essentialism is not entirely useless. We need categories to understand the world. Despite this, strong essentialism used in an unconscious and uncritical way should avoided. We should be aware that all cultural traits of an individual society are time- and context-specific, and that not everyone from the same cultural background is identically influenced by cultural determinants. Age, gender, occupation and other stratification variables all play a role in (re-)forming individuals' identities.

1.6 Understanding Culture: More Appropriate Attitudes

Activity 1-7 From the discussion in the last section, what might be more appropriate attitudes to interpret culture and cultural phenomena?

Dialectical thinking concerns continuous interaction between two opposing factors, through which the contradictions and inconsistencies between them become the driving forces of development (Peng & Nisbett, 1999). Through stressing contradiction, dialectic thinking views things as changing, changeable, and interrelated with each other.

In this book, a dialectical methodology is proposed to interpret culture and cultural phenomena. That is, rather than viewing culture as comprising pre-given and fixed external realities, we perceive culture as open and changeable on the one hand, but by no means free-floating on the other. For example, Eastern and Western cultures are not to be regarded as encapsulated or independent, but, rather, as interdependent and permeable to each other.

Furthermore, the concept of culture is approached as a verb rather than a noun, stressing culture formation, maintenance and development as on-going processes. Culture, on the one hand, is undergoing a constant procedure of transformation, during which certain aspects of the given culture are strengthened while others are challenged, resisted or redefined. On the other hand, changes of culture could be temporarily closed in human history. Otherwise, no cultural codes could have been transmitted to members of any culture group, and all societies would have been universally the same.

Finally, we reject the equation of "one culture=one set of constitutive meanings". On the contrary, social and cultural structures are multi-layered and complicated. In history, apparently isolated societies were marked by significant internal differences. In an era of global cooperation and competition, the scope and speed of cultural diversity and change have been dramatically accelerated. This requires anyone involving in intercultural communication consciously to put aside biased preconceptions, avoid over-generalizing from individual cases, submit to the unexpected and emergent, and continuously seek deepened understandings of cultural phenomena (Holliday, 2004).

1.7 Chapter Summary

Culture is important to us, influencing our behaviors, values, and emotions. It is, however, difficult to define. In this chapter, we have reviewed sociologists', anthropologists', and critical theorists' definitions of culture. We have then discussed the differences between the three interrelated concepts, i.e. culture, race, and ethnicity. By analyzing problems of ethnocentric and strong essentialist views of culture, the chapter has proposed a dialectical methodology in interpreting and analyzing culture and cultural phenomena. While stressing the sharing of cultural codes among members of cultural groups, the dialectical methodology challenges the practices that see culture as static, simplistic, and deterministic. It opens room for exploration of dynamics and complexities of intercultural communication.

1.8 Case Study Assignment

The following excerpt was taken from Liu Yizheng's *The History of Chinese Culture*. Liu Yizheng was a prominent educator in China. His work, *The History of Chinese Culture*, is a comprehensive and systematic examination of Chinese culture from ancient times to the late Qing Dynasty, highly valued for its academic rigor and extensive citations. Please read the excerpt and write a 300-word essay on your understanding and reflection on the excerpt.

> 吾书凡分三编：第一编，自邃古以迄两汉，是为吾国民族本其创造之力，由部落而建设国家，构成独立之文化之时期；第二编，自东汉以迄明季，是以印度文化输入吾国，与吾国固有文化由抵牾而融合之时期；第三编，自明季迄今日，是为中印两种文化均已就衰，而远西之学术、思想、宗教、政法以次输入，相激相荡而卒相合之时期。此三期者，初无截然划分之界限，特就其蝉联蜕化之际，略分畛畔，以便寻绎。实则吾民创造之文化，富于弹性，自古迄今，纚纚相属，虽间有盛衰之判，固未尝有中绝之时……
>
> 柳诒徵《中国文化史》

References

Avruch, K. (1998). *Culture and conflict resolution.* United States Institute of Peace Press.

Browne, K. (2011). *An introduction to sociology.* Polity Press.

Buciek, K. (2003). Postcolonial reason-selected perspectives of writing postcolonial geographies. *Nordisk Samhällsgeografisk Tidsskrift, 37,* 9.

Collier, M.J., Hedge, R.S., Lee, W., Nakayama, T. K., & Yep, G. A. (2002). Dialogue on the edges. In M. J. Collier (Ed.), *Transforming communication about culture* (pp. 219–280). Sage.

Ferraro, G. (1998). *The cultural dimension of international business.* Prentice Hall.

Gans, H. J. (1999). *Popular culture and high culture: An analysis and evaluation of taste.* Basic Books.

Geertz, C. (1973). *The interpretation of cultures: Selected essays.* Basic Books.

Hofstede, G. (1991). *Cultures and organizations: Software of the mind.* McGraw-Hill.

Holliday, A. (2004). *Intercultural communication: An advanced resource book.* Routledge.

Komarovsky, M., & Sargent, S. (1949). Research into subcultural influences upon personality. In S. Sargent (Ed.), *Culture and personality* (pp. 143–159). Viking Fund.

Kroeber, A. L., Kluckhohn, C. (1952). *Culture: A critical review of concepts and definitions.* Vintage.

Martin, J., Nakayama, T. (2009). *Intercultural communication in contexts.* McGraw-Hill.

Matsumoto, D. (1996). *Culture and psychology*. Brooks Cole.

Peng, K., Nisbett, R. (1999). Culture, dialectics and reasoning about contradiction. *American Psychologist, 54*(9), 741–754. https://doi.org/10.1037//0003-066x.54.9.741

Schein, E. (1984). Coming to a new awareness of organizational culture. *Sloan Management Review, 25*(2), 3–16.

Spencer-Oatey, H., & Franklin, P. (2009). *Intercultural interaction: A multidisciplinary approach to intercultural communication*. Palgrave.

Therous, P. (1988). *Riding the iron rooster: By train through China*. Penguin.

Triandis, H. C., Lambert, W., & Berry, J. W. (1980). *Handbook of cross-cultural psychology*. Allyn & Bacon.

Williams, R. (1983). *Keywords: A vocabulary of culture and society*. Oxford University Press.

2 Comparing Origins of Civilizations

Peng Fengling

Civilization did not appear overnight. It is a complex way of life that came about as people began to develop urban settlements. This process may take thousands even millions of years.

There are several important stages in the development of civilizations. The first two stages were probably the invention of primitive weapons and the discovery of fire, although nobody knows exactly when human beings acquired the skills of using fire. After that, language was invented. Archeologists had controversial ideas about the sequence of picture language and oral language. Some thought picture language preceded oral language, others proposed oral language appeared before picture language, and some suggested the two developed side by side. Whatever the sequence, the invention of language has been the most important single factor in the development of civilization. A man could draw a picture on the wall of his cave to show in which direction he had gone, or what prey he hoped to catch. With oral language, he could communicate more effectively about daily activities.

The next two important stages were the domestication of animals and the invention of agriculture. Before the invention of agriculture, men were hunters. They went out every day. Sometimes they killed animals, and sometimes animals killed them. Life was difficult and dangerous. Women had to go out every day, too. The invention of agriculture enabled women to stay at home and look after the children and animals. Then their husbands did not have to go hunting for meat. They could stay at home and build villages and cities. As a result, civilization began.

The early civilizations began around 3000 BCE, when the rise of agriculture provided people with sufficient food, and they did not have to spend all their time and energy hunting for meat. At the same time, with surplus food in store, they could exchange and get what they did not have from other tribes. As a result, they had leisure time to think about and do other things rather than just struggled for survival. Therefore, agriculture was a step in human progress to which there was nothing comparable until the machine age, as it made possible an immense increase in human population in the regions where crops could be successfully planted. At first, agriculture could only be practiced in places where nature fertilized the soil after each harvest, and agriculture met with violent resistance from the pastoral nomads, but the agricultural way of life prevailed in the end because of the physical comforts it provided. As farming skills developed, agricultural populations advanced beyond village life, and many people no longer had to practice farming at all. They shifted energy and attention to other businesses, such as art, music, philosophy, and so on. As a result, civilizations advanced.

Another fundamental advance in the development of civilization was writing, which made it possible to keep records and transmit information to people who were not present when the information was given.

To summarize, these inventions and discoveries, including weapons, fire, speech, domesticating animals, agriculture, and writing, made the existence of civilized communities possible. From the emergence of early civilizations until the beginning of the Industrial Revolution, there was no technical advance comparable to these. During this long period, man had time to become accustomed to his technique, and to develop the beliefs and political organizations appropriate to it.

2.1 Origins of Chinese and Western Civilizations

All advanced societies that populate the modern world have humble origins. At the initial stage of civilization, agriculture was confined to areas where water resources were plentiful. Water, in the form of lakes, seas, and especially rivers, played an essential role in the development of civilizations. Water provided a steady supply of drinking water, and made the land fertile for growing crops. Moreover, goods and people could be transported easily on water, and people could hunt animals that came to drink water and catch fish in the rivers. As time went by, survival requirements called for people wandering in the wildness to travel downstream, where centers of human population tended to concentrate. Consequently, some civilizations originated from great rivers, such as Chinese civilization, Egyptian civilization, Mesopotamian civilization and so on, while other civilizations originated from seas, such as the ancient Greek civilization. According to Clayton and Dent, the former type of civilization is termed as a river civilization, which is an agricultural nation or civilization originated along a river, while the latter is termed as a sea civilization, which developed around seas (Clayton & Dent, 1973).

2.1.1 Origin of Chinese civilization

Chinese civilization originated in various regional centers along both the Yellow River and Yangtze River valleys in the Neolithic era. The great amount of archeological information available about ancient Chinese civilization tells us that Chinese ways of life were greatly influenced by the Yellow River and Yangtze River. The Yellow River, in particular, is essential to the development of Chinese civilization. As the Chinese regard yellow as an emblem of loess land, the emperor, the yellow skin, and the legendary Chinese dragon, the overwhelming Yellow River is referred to not only as a river, but also a symbol of the Chinese nation. For thousands of years, the Yellow River has been known as the "mother river" of Chinese nation and the "cradle of Chinese civilization".

As the Yellow River traces a source high up the majestic Kunlun Mountain in the far west to the immense Pacific Ocean, it drains a basin of 795,000 sq km, which has been the most prosperous region in early Chinese history. Relics about the Neolithic Age, Bronze Age, Iron Age and the like have been discovered in the drainage of the river. The stories of three cultural heroes are well known: Suiren Shi[1] who taught the Chinese to make fire by drilling wood, Fuxi[2] who invented hunting, trapping and fishing, and Shennong[3] (also known as the Red Emperor or Yan Emperor) who contributed immensely to the establishment of agriculture. It is believed that the three legendary individuals began the development of civilization in the Yellow River basin.

Around 4000 BCE the Yellow River civilization began in China. From

---

1. Suiren Shi: 燧人氏。
2. Fuxi: 伏羲。
3. Shennong: 神农，也被称为炎帝。

4000 BCE to 2000 BCE (Xu, 2004), many ethnic groups and civilizations also emerged. But unfortunately in later time, some of them intermitted, some went to a low tide, and only Yellow River civilization developed itself into a higher level. From the Xia Dynasty (ca. 2070–ca. 1600BCE) to the Tang Dynasty (618–907), the Yellow River area was always the center of politics, economy, science and technology as well as culture.

2.1.2 Origin of Western civilization

Western civilization is not a geographically defined concept. In a general term, it pertains to the civilization which appeared first in Mesopotamia at the Tigris[1] and Euphrates River[2] basins in present-day Iraq and Iran, a region that Westerners today call the Middle East, and generally spread westwards. In its broader sense, its roots may be traced back to 9000 BCE, when humans existing in hunter-gatherer societies began to settle into agricultural societies. However, Western civilization in its more strictly defined European sphere traces its roots back to classical antiquity. From European and Mediterranean origins, it has spread to produce the dominant cultures of modern North America, South America, and much of Oceania, and has had immense global influence in recent centuries.

At every stage of its growth, Western civilization drew heavily on the heritages of oriental civilizations in Egypt, Asia Minor[3], the Middle East, the Indus, and China. However, to define the birthplace of Western civilization, the answer should be ancient Greece. The ancient Greeks made magnificent achievements in government, science, philosophy, and the arts, which were the most significant starting point of Western civilization.

Since 2000 BCE, Crete started to have early countries, which formed the famous Crete civilization (Xu, 2004). The Aegean civilization had a profound influence on ancient Greek and Roman civilization: It was the cradle of Western civilization. During 1100 BCE and 900 BCE, the most important cultural heritage was the Homeric epics. The epics included the legend and culture of the Mycenaean civilization period as well as the reflection of the temporal social situation. After 800 BCE when the Aegean age faded, the Greeks rebuilt their country through extensive oversea colonial movements. At that time, the country was centered on one city, combined with surrounding villages. In 431 BCE outburst the Peloponnesian War, which

---

1. Mesopotamia: 美索不达米亚平原; Tigris: 底格里斯河。
2. Euphrates River: 幼发拉底河。
3. Asia Minor: 小亚细亚。

ended the Classical age and led Greece into crisis and became the capture of Macedonia. Later in the classical period, the city-states suffered from internal and external conflicts, then entered the Macedonia period. In 338 EBC, Macedonia completely dominated the Greeks.

The ancient Greeks made great achievements in philosophy, mathematics, history, academy, architecture, astronomy, and so on. Its contribution to Western and human civilization is prominent.

2.2 Differences Between Chinese and Western Civilizations

This section will explore the differences between Chinese and Western civilizations from the perspectives of geographical features, peripheral historical and cultural environments, and the mode of economies and societies.

2.2.1 River civilization vs. sea civilization

Since the Yellow River is the cradle of Chinese civilization, while the Aegean Sea breeds Western civilization, we will first explore the geographical environments of the Chinese and Western civilizations.

Chinese civilization began within the Yellow River Valley. The Yellow River, with the length of 5,464 km, is the northernmost major Chinese river, the second longest river in China and the sixth longest in the world. Directly to the south is the Yangtze River.

The name of the Yellow River can be indicative of its characteristics. Why is it called "yellow"? Because the water contains a large amount of mud. As the saying goes, "One bowl of water, half a bowl of mud". The Yellow River's maximum annual sediment transport may reach 4.39 billion tons. In an ordinary year, the Yellow River produces 1.6 billion tons of sediment, of which 400 million tons remain in the lower reaches for years, forming alluvial plains that are conducive to planting.

After years and years of scouring and dozens of diversions, the topography along the Yellow River varied greatly, with a vast land of lofty plateau, large plains, rolling land, and big and small basins surrounded by lofty mountains. Such varied topography was favorable for the development of agriculture, and different types of crops could be grown.

The climate along this area was also diverse: from subtropical in the south to subarctic in the north. Monsoon winds, caused by differences in the heat-absorbing capacity of the continent and the ocean, dominated the climate. Alternating seasonal air-mass movements and accompanying winds were moist in summer and dry in winter. The advance and retreat of the monsoons accounted in a large degree for the timing of the rainy season and the amount of rainfall throughout the country. Tremendous differences in latitude, longitude, and altitude gave rise to sharp variations in precipitation and temperature. However, most of the country lay in the temperate belt, which provided favorable conditions for the development of an agricultural civilization.

Compared with the stormy seas, rivers are generally milder and more stable. Over the years, when people lived along rivers long enough, they gradually accumulated adequate knowledge about the flows and overflows of rivers, and their lives became stable and predictable. When they predicted the overflow of rivers, they could move away temporarily. When the overflow ended, they could then move back. The flood usually left a fertile alluvial plain where crops could grow well. As a result, in the thousands of years of evolution, in the Chinese river civilization, people are gentle, peaceful and inclusive. They do not like expansion or aggression; instead, they live and work in peace and contentment, entirely satisfied with their state of life.

Different from the Chinese river civilization, Western civilization developed around the Aegean Sea, showing characteristics different from Chinese civilization. Unlike the prosperous floodplains of rivers, Greece was a barren world of mountains and sea. Only 10% of the rugged terrain of Greece was flat, and the islands that dotted the Aegean and Ionian seas nurtured the development of small, self-contained agricultural societies. Greek weather was volatile, constantly threatening farmers with failure. Rainfall varied enormously from year to year, and arid summers alternated with cool, wet winters. Wheat, barley, and beans were the main crops of Greek life. Farmers struggled to produce the Mediterranean triad of grains, olives, and wine, which first began to dominate agriculture around 3000 BCE.

However, such unfavorable agricultural conditions could not sustain an affluent life, as people could not live on olive oil or wine only. They had to seek other means of livelihood in order to live well and live better. What was worse, the yields from land were unable to support an ever-growing population. As a result, they had to try other means to exchange their agricultural products with people from other places, they had to grasp more land and more materials to survive, and they had to turn their eyes to other places for better opportunities. Fortunately, Constant fluctuations in climate and weather from region to region helped to counterbalance the geographical isolation and low agricultural yields by forcing insular communities to build contacts with a wider world to survive.

Due to the proximity of the sea to most Greek city-states, ancient Greeks became a sea-going people. They became merchants and traders and developed a sense of freedom and independence not seen before. The Mediterranean Sea provided reliable shipping routes linking Asia, Africa, and Europe, along which political and religious ideas could be traded along with raw materials such as timber, copper, tin, gold, and silver as well as agricultural produce and necessities such as wine, olive oil, grain, and livestock. The acquirement of sailing and navigation knowledge and skills helped the Ancient Greeks to reach out, explore, and communicate with the outside world. By 3100 BCE, the Egyptians were employing sails on boats on the Nile River. The subsequent development of the technology, coupled with knowledge of the wind and stars allowed naval powers such as the Greeks, Phoenicians, Carthaginians, and Romans to navigate long distances and control large areas by commanding the sea. Cargo galleys often employed slave oarsmen to power their ships and slavery was an important feature of the ancient Western economy. Gradually, the great ancient capitals were linked, such as the city of Athens, home to Athenian democracy, and the Greek philosophers Aristotle, Plato, and Socrates; the city of Jerusalem, the Jewish capital, where Jesus preached and was executed around 3 AD; and the city of Rome, which gave rise to the Roman Empire and later encompassed much of Western Europe and the Mediterranean area.

In general, the ancient Greek civilization has the characteristics of openness, expansion, diversity, and multicenter. These features of sea civilization make it distinct from the Chinese civilization, which is gentle, peaceful and defensive, homogenous, continuous, self-reclusive, and conservative.

2.2.2 Agricultural civilization vs. trading civilization

Every society, every civilization, depends on economic, technological, biological, and demographic circumstances. Material and biological conditions always help determine the destiny of civilizations. Due to the different geographical environments, there were considerable differences between the two civilizations in the process of development. The different geographical environments and diverse natural resources were the natural basis of human division of labor, which led to different types of material production modes. They in turn resulted in the differences in culture, and directly affected the lifestyles and ways of thinking of people in various regions.

For a long time, people were the only major force of civilization development. A rise or fall in the population, health or illness, economic or technological growth or decline, all deeply affect the cultural as well as the social structure. An increase in population always helped the growth of civilization. However, when the population grew faster than the economy, what was once an advantage became a drawback. The results were famines, falls in real earnings, popular uprisings, and grim periods of slump, until epidemics and starvation together brutally thinned out the serried ranks of human beings. After such biological disasters, the survivors briefly had an easier time and expansion began again, at increasing speed until the next setback.

Boasting one of the most glorious agricultural civilizations, agriculture began in remote antiquity when there was still no written history. In one of the ancient Chinese legends, there was a story of Shen Nong Shi concerning the origin of agriculture. Before Shen Nong Shi, people ate reptiles, little animals, mussels, and wild vegetables. As the population gradually increased, food gradually became less sufficient, thereby creating a desperate need to explore new means of food. Shennong tasted all kinds of herbals, even poisons, to finally select the grains that could be eaten by people. Later, he also studied the climate and invented some farming tools, which led to the appearance of husbandry in China.

While the legend leaves behind some clues about when agriculture originated in China, modern archeology has provided more abundant and reliable materials about the origin and condition of Chinese agriculture. So far, there have been thousands of discoveries of agricultural sites during the Neolithic Age all across China, especially along the Yellow River and the Yangtze River.

Sometime around 4000 BCE, when the area was much more temperate and forested, populations around the southern bend of the Yellow River began to practice agriculture. They sowed millet and later people began cultivating rice in the south, near the Huai River. There was a Neolithic, tribal people who used stone tools. They domesticated animals very early while still continued hunting. Remains of game animals were almost as common as domestic animals in these villages.

Excavation of a Peiligang culture site in Xinzheng County, Henan Province[1], found a community that flourished around 6000–5500 BCE, with evidence of agriculture, constructed buildings, pottery, and burial of the dead. With agriculture came increased population, the ability to store and redistribute crops, and the potential to support specialist craftsmen and administrators (Pringle, 1998, pp.1446–1450). In late Neolithic times, the Yellow River valley began to establish itself as a center of Yangshao culture[2] 7,000 to 5,000 years ago, and the first villages were founded; the most archaeologically significant of these was found at Banpo[3]. Later, Yangshao culture was superseded by the Longshan culture[4], which was also centered on the Yellow River about 5,000 years ago (Xu, 2004, p. 40).

The development of agriculture and the domestication of animals allowed people to stay in one spot instead of wandering from place to place following their main food source—animals. Some Neolithic people learned how to plant and raise crops and keep and raise livestock for food. Now people were put in the situation of living together permanently. As a result, much cooperation was needed for survival and civilizations started to grow. As agricultural productivity increased, fewer people were needed to work in the fields producing food. These people who were not needed could then become artisans, merchants, or traders and production of all sorts was able to increase, thereby providing a better standard of living for all.

During its long history, China invented metal smelting technology, irrigation projects, and intensive and meticulous farming. They gradually established a set of agricultural technologies, including furrowing, harrowing, and leveling land, and invented sophisticated farming tools. Around 533–544, an agricultural encyclopedia titled *Important Arts for People's Welfare*[5] by famous agronomist Jia Sixie summarized previous agricultural experiences. Highlighted by the invention of farming tools and skills, Chinese society, politics, technology, and culture experienced substantial improvements, which in turn propelled the development of agriculture.

This mode of life to a large extent contributed to the type of civilization

---

1. 位于河南省新郑市的裴李岗文化遗址。
2. 仰韶文化。
3. 在陕西省西安市东郊半坡村发现的一处仰韶文化遗址。
4. 龙山文化，在黄河中下游地区发展形成的文化遗存。
5. 《齐民要术》，我国古代北魏时期贾思勰著。

and culture. The Chinese thus became a sedentary people with a highly developed agriculture. They were tied to the farming land and largely dependent on the land. In spring the seeds were sown, in summer crops grew, in autumn crops were harvested, and in winter harvests were stored for use in the coming year. This agricultural civilization is characterized by stability, self-sufficiency, self-content, harmony among people, and harmony between nature and human beings.

Geography also had a great influence on Greece and its inhabitants. It was largely responsible for numerous continuities in its extensive history. While the mountains that split the Greek lands contributed to localism, they had been a major barrier to unity as a nation as well. The struggle for communication by land and the significant presence of the sea made mariners out of the Greeks for numerous generations.

In ancient Greece, many cities had land that was used for farming within the city, but most of the people lived in small towns and villages outside of the city. The Greeks had their private space that consisted of the agricultural fields in the territory of the polis and their houses compacted in settlements, whether in the central town of the city-state, in smaller towns, or in villages. People preferred to live in such compacted settlements, even when agriculture was their main source of support. There has been occasional evidence of how agricultural land was organized by the residents of the settlements in rectangular and equal lots. The idea was that each family would farm a single plot of land. However, there was a tendency for farmland to become divided and for a landowner to own many plots of land scattered all over the community.

Therefore, the small peasant economy did not become the normal state of Greek society as in China. Scarce food production could not support a larger population, and hills and mountains cut up the few remaining plains, preventing the Greek peninsula from being truly united, which eventually led to the formation of large city-states on the Greek peninsula. The population of city-states was relatively sparse. Until the 6th century BC, there were hundreds of city-states on the Greek peninsula, the smallest of which was not more than a few tens of kilometers, and the largest was several thousand kilometers.

Due to the enormous mountains and limited farmland, farming alone could not support a growing population. Ancient Greeks had to turn to the forests and seas for a living. In addition to stock farming and fishery, trading and emigration developed into the major means of living. In addition, as the Mediterranean climate was not conducive to the growth of crops, but favorable to the growth of commercial crops, including grapes and olives, the Greeks made wine out of grapes, pressed olive oil, and sold them in exchange for food and other products. As a result, the handicraft industry was developed along with trading. Handicraft industry and trading were interdependent and inter-promoted, which not only enhanced the economy of Greece, but also strengthened the link between Greece and other regions.

What allowed the Greek peninsula to carry out such a large volume of traffic was the large number of ports. The coastline of the Greek peninsula was jagged, and many places were excellent natural harbors. The city-states bordering the sea had their ports for trade. The long coastline and natural harbors provided unique conditions for the development of trading.

Outside the circle of Greek civilization itself, Greece was not alone. As a civilization that encompassed three continents, Europe, Asia, and Africa, Ancient Greece communicated with ancient Egypt in Africa and the Persian Empire in Central Asia. The Greek peninsula was at the intersection of North Africa and Central Asia, and the intersection of two great civilizations made Ancient Greece a transportation hub.

Around 3000 BCE, in the Mediterranean world of the eastern Aegean Sea, the prosperous Minoan civilization began a close relationship with Asia and Africa, and was deeply influenced by West Asian and Egyptian civilization (Xu, 2004). The trading provided bronze ware, jewelry, and ivory accessories to Greece. At the same time, due to west Asia social unrest, many goods were exported to Greece, and quite a number of craftsmen came to the Greek world to seek a way of living.

Such communication and contact had an immeasurable influence on Greek civilization. Many business centers were established by ancient Greeks, not only in west Asia, but also in the land of Egypt, the Nile tributaries, and other places. Since then, the prominent centers have became the bridge between Greece and other Mediterranean countries. This tradition of trading, undoubtedly, cultivated the Western commercial culture.

In summary, the survival crisis forced the ancient Greeks to develop an innovative spirit. Its natural mission was to explore overseas markets, seize colonies, and expand overseas. Moreover, because business involved traveling, it was necessary to find partners with excellent physical and intellectual abilities rather than family members. As a result, the blood relationship structure was broken down, while theological and legal systems were established. The Greek civilization emphasized social contract, which weakened the blood ties but strengthened the legal system. Furthermore, benefits gained from trade were many times more than harvests gained from agriculture, people were accustomed to the thinking mode of gaining the greatest benefits from the least costs. All these characteristics made ancient Greek civilization a trading civilization, which is different from the Chinese agricultural civilization.

2.2.3 Family-state[1] vs. city-state

Based on the agricultural mode of life, Chinese society established a predominant nature-based, farm-based economy. This was the economic foundation of the feudal system. The peasants, who made up over 90% of the population, produced and made nearly everything for themselves, not for the market. They grew rice, wheat or corn, and vegetables, and they also raised pigs, goats, and chickens. They grew cotton and hemp and wove very coarse cloth with their handlooms. They made their own tools, furniture, and other things they used. In short, there were very few things that they had to buy from shops in town.

This type of economy in turn strengthened the blood tie among family members. Family was important. The authority of the family belonged to the father. However, a family could not be separated from the clan. The clan system was a large social group composed of several families, whose members usually had the same ancestors, surnames, ancestral temples, clan rules, and were bound by the patriarchal system. The clan system originated from the same ancestors and was characterized by genealogies, ancestral halls, clan fields, patriarchs and rules. In the clan system, the genealogy was formulated to prevent disorder, the ancestral halls were built as places for sacrificial activities to enhance family cohesion, the clan fields were purchased to maintain clan's public expenditure and economic base, the chiefs were assigned to be responsible for management and decision-making, and clan rules were made to regulate the clan behaviors. The clan system played a controlling role in the rural society, stabilizing the social order, and implementing social control and autonomy by means of clan rules and clan laws.

---

1. 将家天下译成 family-state 是为了和 city-state 相对应。家天下通常可被翻译为 imperial family 或 family-governed monarch country。

In combination with the clan system, the patriarchal system also played an essential role in the ancient Chinese society. The patriarchal system was also based on blood relationship, characterized by the combination of clan organization and state organization, and the consistency of patriarchal level and political level in political hierarchy. The patriarchal system, which originated in the late primitive society, took shape in the Xia Dynasty, developed in the Shang Dynasty, and was well established in the Zhou Dynasty, had an impact on the subsequent dynasties. It was mainly implemented through the enfeoffment system, in which the emperor enfeoffed the princes, and the princes enfeoffed the officials, eventually forming a patriarchal system from the central to the local.

The patriarchal system and the clan system were two sets of complementary social mechanisms in ancient Chinese society. The patriarchal system started from the top-level political structure and established the inheritance and ruling order based on blood relationship, while the clan system started more from the grassroots society and realized social control and cultural inheritance through family organization. Together, they built a traditional social structure with blood ties, distinct layers and relative stability, which contributed to the establishment of a unified empire.

During the Western Zhou (1046-771 BCE) or Eastern Zhou (770-256 BCE) dynasties, Chinese society entered the kingdom stage. Since the Qin (221-207 BCE) and Han (202BCE-220 CE) dynasties, China implemented the system of prefectures and counties, which was an effective centralized system and strengthened the direct control of the central government over the localities. Thus a unified empire was established. This social system lasted for more than 2,000 years until it was shaken by foreign cannons during the Opium War. In this political system, the country was governed more or less in the same way. There were modifications from dynasty to dynasty in the organizations and workings of the government, but very few fundamental changes in the main structure of the political system. All powers were held in the hands of the emperor, who was assisted by a group of ministers led by the prime minister. Scholars who had passed certain examinations were given government posts. This system suited the social conditions on the whole. Except in wars or great political upheavals, the country was effectively governed, and law and order were maintained.

In a unified empire, the centralization system was conducive to the unification of laws, writing, weights and measures, promoted the integration of different ethnic groups and regions, and formed a unified concept of the Chinese nation. The idea of "great unity" in China emphasized the idea that the world was one family and peace was the most valuable, that a unified leader and central government would lead to social stability and national prosperity.

Different from the Chinese empire, the ancient Greece developed a different political system, the city-state or polis. The hills and mountains of the Greek peninsula were relatively rugged, making it difficult for the early peoples of Greece to travel overland. This geographical factor resulted in three important impacts on the lives of the ancient Greeks.

First, the rugged terrain made it difficult for a common Greek empire to unit all Greek-speaking people. Instead, people established separate city-states. Second, due to the rugged terrain, there was relatively little cultural diffusion among the city-states. Each of them had its own distinct form of government and culture. Athens and Sparta were two excellent examples of completely different systems. Third, the rugged terrain forced the Greeks to turn out to the sea for trade and food production. Thus they became great sailors, fishermen, and traders, trading with many other great civilizations in existence at that time, such as Ancient Egypt, Scythia, Mesopotamia and Phoenicia.

Among the many city-states founded by the ancient Greeks, Athens was the most influential and most typical, which was known for its democracy, economic development, and cultural prosperity. The city-state of Athens was located on the Attica Peninsula in central Greece and was mainly inhabited by Ionians and Akkaya people. The land was mountainous, rich in minerals; the coastline twisted, with many good ports, but there was not much good land for farming. In general, the geographical environment was suitable for the development of navigation, handcraft industry and trading, but not conducive to agricultural development. Around 700 BCE, a unified city-state centered on the city of Athens took form.

The citizens of Athens were made up of nobles and commoners. At the beginning of the city-state, aristocracy was practiced, and the original clan aristocracy held political and economic privileges. With the growing economic strength of the new industrial and commercial class, the desire to break the exclusive power of the gentile aristocracy was becoming stronger and stronger. Together with other commoners, they launched a struggle for power against the gentile aristocracy, and the result of the struggle led Athens to embark on the road of ancient democracy.

Gradually, the Athenian government developed into a direct democracy, in which all citizens voted on major issues instead of electing representatives to do it for them. As a result, this governmental system required frequent meetings of the Athenians to vote on important issues. These meetings often entailed debates among citizens over policy decisions, such as going to war against another city-sate. Athens' direct democracy served as an important step toward individual freedom and involvement of individuals in the decision-making process of the government. However, only those over the age of 18 could vote, while slaves and women could not vote, hold office, or inherit property.

Sparta was another typical example of the ancient Greek city-states. Around 800 BCE, the primitive commune of Sparta disintegrated, and gradually formed a set of distinctive social and political systems of city-states. Sparta was known for its harsh discipline, dictatorship, and militarism. In the process of expansion and conquest, the Spartans turned native people into slaves, forced them to work on the land and engaged in hard agricultural labor. Each year, the slaves submitted more than half of their harvest to the slave owners, while they themselves lived a miserable life. However, Spartan women were surprisingly well treated. Women were almost equal to men, and they could remarry while their husbands were at war. They could take part in various activities, study and exercise, because the Spartans wanted women to be as strong as men so as to deliver strong children.

Sparta's government was basically an oligarchy, a government controlled by a small group of people. Power was in the hands of a few aristocrats. Often at meetings the group able to shout the loudest would be the ones who won a vote or had their policy accepted. The Spartan government was mostly concerned with ensuring that the city-state had a powerful military machine to protect itself from outside invasion and to conquer others. The government also forbade its citizens to travel abroad and did not often accept visitors. They feared that contact with outside would weaken the discipline of the population. Babies that did not appear strong were often discarded. Above all, the Spartans valued strength and virility over intellect and academic achievement.

In summary, based on the agricultural civilization, Chinese society established a clan system and patriarchal, which contributed to the establishment of a unified empire. As one of the major contributors to

Western civilization, the Aegean civilization provided the prototype for later forms of Western society. Due to the barren land, isolated hills and proximity to the Aegean Sea, the ancient Greeks became a sea-going people who relied heavily on trading. Based on this trading civilization, Greeks established city-states, which showed some characteristics of the Western society.

2.3 Origin and Development of Civilizations

As discussed above, the essential characteristics of a civilization depend on the constraints or advantages of its geographical environment. If we assume that all human achievements involved challenge and response, and that nature had to present itself as a difficulty to overcome, when humans took up the challenge, their response would lay the foundations of civilization.

Responses to natural challenges continually freed humanity from its environment and at the same time subjected it to the resultant solutions. In this sense, can we conclude that the geographical environment was the major element that promoted or restricted culture creation?

Scholars holding the cultural-ecology viewpoint emphasize the role of the physical environment as one powerful determinant of customs, lifestyles, and behaviors in different cultures. Some cultural ecologists adopt a strong version of culture environment relations, advocating that environmental phenomena are responsible in some manner for the origin or development of cultural behavior under investigation. In this approach, the environment is seen as strongly determining, limiting and affecting behavior and cultural processes.

However, with the development of science, we now ascertain that the geographical environment is not the utmost element in deciding the path of cultures. However, we deem that the geographical conditions and differences resulted, in the first place, the different ethnical characters and cultural spirits, especially in the formation stage of a culture. During this period, geographical conditions, such as the beaches, deserts, prairies, rivers, and climate, the mode of production and life based on these conditions, as well as the relations of a certain area with neighboring areas, were likely to affect the development direction of a culture. When a culture develops to a certain stage, the gradually mature intellectual factors begin to play a more important role, resulting in a conscious choice of culture.

2.4 Chapter Summary

In Chinese history, the Yellow River is not simply a set of characters on a page and the name of a river. In fact, millennia ago the Chinese civilization emerged from the central region of this basin. The land in the basin was rich, and the farmers needed the rivers for growing crops and for transportation. Meantime, the source of rich land was new soil deposited each year when the rivers flooded. So farmers were also worried about flood. This caused them to focus on the control of floods and to exploit the potential of the land. Therefore, in a sense, the rivers provided water for farming crops which had become a catalyst for the growth of civilization. The development of agriculture helped people develop specialized trades or crafts. Based on this agricultural civilization, Chinese society developed a feudal system which emphasized family ties, patriarchy and royalty.

As one of the major contributors to Western civilization, ancient Greek civilization provided the prototype for later forms of Western society. Intellectual and cultural achievements, together with social and economic developments in ancient Greece and its neighboring areas, marked the beginning of Western civilization and the ending of the barbarous age in Europe. Due to the barren land and isolated mountainous topological conditions, ancient Greece developed city-state, which was different from the Chinese family-state.

2.5 Case Study Assignments

Assignment 2-1 Read the following passage concerning the origin of Chinese civilization and answer the questions.

> In the *Book of Changes (Zhouyi)*, there is a line which states that "the original book comes from the Yellow River and Luo River, and then the saints followed it". In the *Biography of Emperors (Diwang Shiji)*, when speaking about the origin of culture, there are stories of fish, dragons, tortoises, and phoenixes. For example, *Quotes for the Beginners (Chuxueji)* quoted the *Biography of Emperors* to state that "the graphic book comes from the fish movements". *The Carving Jade Collection (Diaoyuji)* quoted the *Biography of Emperors*, to say that "the tortoise in the Luo River carried the book out, and the dragon in the Yellow River brought the painting". *The Collection of Good Fortunes (Jirui)* also quoted the *Biography of Emperors* that "the

phoenix carried the painting and put it in front of the emperor". If we believe that in mythological time, there was the concept of a "totem" existing in ancient Chinese history, then we can say that different cultures from different tribes gradually converged into the mainstream of Chinese culture, just as Wen Yiduo said in *The Study of Fuxi* (*Fuxikao*) that *"the convergence of totems is the only way of a totem society development"*. In this process, *"when different totems blended into a complex"* he said, *"a blended totem is born from the merger of different tribes, ancient Egypt being a good example"*. In Chinese history, the northern constellation *Xuanwu* originally depicted two separate animals, the tortoise, and the snake, but now it has become the blending of a tortoise and snake. Something is different here in the blending of the totems, however, in that, after those totems are blended, each animal remains unchanged. But with the Chinese dragon, after the melding of different totems, there was developed a totally new one, and the former smaller totem ceased to exist at all. Therefore, the former example can be called the "blended totem", while the latter can be called the "mixed totem".

Obviously, from examining these ancient Chinese cultures, one can see that at the time when primitive cultures were advancing to become more advanced societies, these separate ancient tribes began to merge with one another, which provided the necessary conditions for the birth of modern Chinese civilization.

Concerning the historical analysis of the origin of Chinese civilization, at first the doctrine of "One Central China" was the dominant theory. Gradually historians have developed the multi-origin theory, which is also called the "stars in the sky" theory. It contends that the early people were definitely scattered across the Chinese territory like the stars in the sky.

Su Bingqi pointed out that *"there used to be a viewpoint that the Yellow River was the cradle of all Chinese people, and our culture first developed from there, then spread around; so the cultures of other regions could only rely on it to develop. It is a one-sided view. In our history, the Yellow River area did make a great contribution, and especially in the time of recorded civilization, it has always been a dominant culture. But at the same time, the ancient cultures in other areas were also developing with their own characteristics. The archeological findings in different places have verified this point. Meanwhile, this influence was mutually beneficial, since as central China influenced other regions, it also received influence from other regions".*

Su believed there are six areas that made great contributions to the birth of early Chinese civilization: (1) the area of Shaanxi, Henan, and Shanxi; (2) Shandong and its vicinity; (3) Hubei and its vicinity; (4) the lower reaches of the Yangtze River; (5) Southern China, centered around the Poyang Lake and the Zhujiang River Delta; and (6) Northern China surrounding the Great Wall. Some other scholars combine the one-origin theory and multi-origin theory together to explain the origin of Chinese civilization and its development. They consider that the multifactor distribution and *"the moon supported by the stars"* distribution together formed the Central Plains culture in another sense, which is also the center of the Chinese social and cultural development of our ancestors.

The above analysis is identical to the following conclusion made by Zhang Guangzhi. He stated that *"No matter whether we consider Northern China or Southern China, we can propose a hypothesis that since 4000 BCE, several regional cultures with special features and characteristics connected with each other and formed a sphere of interaction".* He said, *"Moreover, this sphere of interaction formed 4,000 years ago, which stretched to the Liao River in the North, and the Zhujiang River Delta in the South, along the sea coast in the east and Gansu, Qinghai in the West. This can be called the China sphere of interaction or the pre-China sphere of interaction, because this pre-historic sphere formed the geographical center of China, and all of the regional cultures in this sphere played important roles in the formation of Chinese civilization in the time of the Qin and Han dynasties".*

(Zhang, 2015)

Questions:

(1) Do you agree with the viewpoints stated in the above passage?

(2) Please find out more theories on the origin of Chinese civilization, read them, and compare which one is the most solid.

Assignment 2-2 Read the following passage and answer the questions.

> Environmental determinism, also known as geographical determinism, is the view that the physical environment, rather than social conditions, determines culture. Those who believe this view say that humans are strictly defined by stimulus-response (environment-behavior). Below is one of the representative thoughts of environmental determinism.
>
> *"Now the water of Qi is forceful and twisting. Therefore its people are greedy and warlike,"* and *"The water of Chu is gentle, yielding, and pure. Therefore its people are lighthearted, resolute, and sure of themselves."*
>
> (*Works of Guan Zhong*, the chapter "Water and Earth", as cited in Yang, 2010)

Questions:

(1) Is environmental determinism reasonable in any sense?

(2) What are the limitations of environmental determinism?

(3) What do you think is the possible relationship between environment and culture?

References

Clayton, P. A., & Dent, J. (1973). *The ancient river civilizations: Western man & the modern world.* Elsevier.

Pringle, H. (1998). The slow birth of agriculture. *Science, 282*(5393), 1446–1450. https://doi.org/10.1126/science.282.5393.1446

Yang, X. J. (2010). *Nongye de qiyuan yu zhongguo zaoqi wenming de fazhan.* [Origin of agriculture and evolution of Chinese early civilization]. *Journal of Anhui Agriculture Science, 38*(25), 14169–14171. http://10.3969/j.issn.0517-6611.2010.25.229

Zhang, Q. Z. (2015). *An introduction to Chinese history and culture.* Springer.

Ma X., Qi, T. (2023). *Zhongguo gudai xiangcun zongzu yanjiu.* [The study of rural clan in ancient China]. The Commercial Press.

Wang, Z. Z. (2013). *Zhongguo gudai guojia de qiyuan yu wangquan de xingcheng.* [The origin of the state and the formation of kingship in ancient China]. China Social Science Press.

3
Comparing Chinese and Western Philosophy

Peng Fengling

The word "philosophy" comes from the Ancient Greek "philosophia," which literally means "love of wisdom." Philosophy is universally defined as the study of the wisdom or knowledge of general and fundamental problems, facts, and situations connected with human existence, such as those connected with reality, existence, values, reason, mind, language, and so on. Philosophy is distinguished from other ways of addressing such problems by its critical, generally systematic approach and its reliance on rational argument. In more casual speech, by extension, "philosophy" can refer to the most basic beliefs, concepts, and attitudes of an individual or group.

Since ancient times, people have been interested in the fundamental problems of existence and in the answers which human race has sought to find in the long journey of civilization. Studying philosophy helps men to understand their own and other times, shedding light on the ethical, religious, political, legal, economic, and other conceptions of the past and the present, by revealing the underlying principles on which they are based.

Chinese and Western philosophy are two important philosophical traditions, covering thousands of years of intellectual exploration and accumulation of wisdom. Generally, philosophical traditions formed under different cultural backgrounds have distinct characteristics and differences. Chinese and Western philosophy represent different ways of thinking and conceptual systems of the East and the West.

Chinese philosophy has a long and rich history, rooted in the historical and cultural soil of Chinese civilization, including the ideological systems of Confucianism, Taoism, Mohism, Buddhism, legalism, Yangming theory and many others. Western philosophy, on the other hand, originated in ancient Greece and was heavily influenced by Christian theology and medieval philosophy, developing into a unique philosophical system that includes numerous schools and thinkers such as Socrates, Plato, Aristotle, Descartes, Locke, just to name a few.

Numerous Chinese thinkers, philosophers, and scholars have explored the differences between Chinese and Western philosophies from various perspectives, and have reached profound insights and conclusions. The famous ones included Feng Youlan, Jin Yuelin, Wang Guowei, and numerous others.

According to Feng Youlan, Chinese philosophy is different from Western philosophy. Western philosophy focuses on explaining the world with a rational attitude and treating life with a God-believing attitude, while Chinese philosophy lacks epistemological interest and religious belief, and focuses on promoting human rational understanding of the universe and the nature of life. He believed that the differences between Chinese and Western philosophy are reflected in three aspects: philosophical consciousness and religious feelings—the difference of transcendental spirit; the opposition of subject and object and the unity of heaven and man—the difference of attitude towards the universe; positive method and negative method—the difference of intellectual nature in philosophical speculation.

Jin Yuelin also summarized the differences between Chinese and Western philosophy. According to him, the first difference is the relationship between nature and man. Nature or heaven in Chinese philosophy refers to nature which is not divided into subject and object; instead, human beings also belong to nature. The view of "unity of heaven and man" advocates that the subject merges into the object, and the object merges into the subject, so as to achieve the integration of the individual and universe. On the other hand, the West has a strong desire to conquer nature. Though people regard human nature as "mean, cruel, and low," and man as the angelic child of the forest, they always seem to be at war with nature, asserting the right of man to dominate nature. The second difference is logic. Jin argued that the view is completely wrong that Chinese philosophy is illogical and not based on knowledge. Although the logic and epistemological consciousness of Chinese philosophy are not well developed, Chinese philosophy has strong poetic characteristics. The third difference is the view of life. In Chinese philosophy, the view of life is the view of saints. The Chinese, satisfied with their own contentment, hold the view that everything is given and therefore is to be accepted, while the Western world is dominated by a heroic view of life, such as the notion that man is the measure of all things, that things are the composition of feelings, and that understanding determines the nature of nature, all of which are the inevitable products of anthropocentric thought. The fourth difference is the relationship between philosophy and politics. Chinese philosophy has political attributes, and ethics, politics, reflection and knowledge are integrated into a philosopher, in whom knowledge and virtue are inseparable, and politics is the tool for implementing his philosophy; on the contrary, Western philosophy and politics are divided. From Socrates to Aristotle, philosophers emphasize the importance of good politics, and believe individuals can be most fully and naturally developed through the medium of a fair political society.

Since Chinese and Western philosophies are systematic human wisdom, it is impossible to compare the two systems in a comprehensive way. This chapter will compare them from a very superficial and broad view, from the following perspectives, view of the world, view of values, and view of knowledge and truth.

3.1 Knowing Chinese and Western Philosophy

This section will briefly explore the historical and cultural background, and the important schools of Chinese and Western Philosophy.

3.1.1 Chinese philosophy

Chinese philosophy is the intellectual tradition of Chinese culture from the recorded history to the present day. The main philosophical topics of Chinese philosophy were heavily influenced by the ideas of important figures like Laozi, Confucius, Mencius, Mozi, Hanfeizi, Dong Zhongshu, Zhu Xi, Wang Yangming, just to name a few. Chinese culture as a whole has been shaped by the influences of these intellectual leaders. The traditional values emphasize family, respect for the elders, social harmony, and so on. The political and social systems, such as the feudal system and imperial examination system, also have had an important impact on the formation and development of Chinese philosophy. In thousands of year's history, the Chinese have developed numerous schools of thought, which have become important components of Chinese culture and shaped the unique features of Chinese tradition.

The Book of Changes (Zhouyi) is the fundamental resource of Chinese philosophy. Almost all subdivisions of Chinese philosophy, such as political philosophy, metaphysics, epistemology, and even ethics and aesthetics are rooted in the philosophy of *Zhouyi*. The ultimate origin of Chinese philosophical awareness comes from the exclusive thinking paradigm involved in the *Zhouyi* philosophical system. *The Book of Changes* explores the *dao* of *tian* for the purpose to understanding human affairs, political events, metaphysics, epistemology, as well as ethics and aesthetics, emphasizing the changes with the passage of time. *Dao* is the path, the way, the highest truth of the world, the source of all things in the universe, and the basis for the survival of all things in the universe, while *tian* means heaven, nature, natural laws, and super being.

Confucianism was established by the sage, Confucius, whose words and deeds were collected by his disciples and followers in the book *The Analects*, which embodies the philosophical thoughts of Confucius. He held that the most fundamental relationship is between father and son. In *The Analects*, family reverence (filial piety) is taken as the root of human feelings. Confucius also extended his thought of family reverence to social management, and infused his governing principle with morality and ritual propriety (etiquette), which is the basis of humanity (benevolence). Mencius developed the Confucian idea of rule by virtue and put forward the "theory of goodness in nature", which believes that people are born with a tendency to be good and need to develop these tendencies through education and cultivation. For him, the unbarring mind reflects on the fundamental concerns of living existence, which is the starting point of human nature.

The political philosophy of Confucianism advocates benevolent governance and the "kingly way". Benevolent governance means that the people are the foundation of the state, and the ruler should pay attention to the sufferings of the people, implement benevolent policies, including reducing taxes and corvee, protecting the basic needs of the people, and advocating moral education of filial piety and loyalty. In addition, the monarch should be subject to the supervision and choice of the people, and if the monarch is cruel, the people have the right to replace him. The "kingly way" advocates to govern the country by virtue and morality, and opposes to rule by force and strength. The moral responsibility and emotional connection in the relationship between the king and subjects are essential, so that a ruler should treat his people as if they were his own parents, and the people should respect and be close to their ruler.

Daoism explores the *dao* of water to understand personal events. In Daoist thoughts, *dao* is nature, the root of all things, and all things change naturally according to their own nature, so it is not necessary to act in a deliberate way; instead, human beings should act like water, being weak and yielding, so as to prevail over the strong. Daoism also advocates ruling without doing anything. It is the so-called non-action and governance without interference, which means lenient punishment and simplified administration, rest, and recuperation. Officials do nothing and the people are self-oriented, and the ruler does nothing and the subjects do something. Daoism proposes emptying the heart. As *dao* is empty, one should remove thoughts in the mind in order to be happy; one should have no worries in order to experience the joy of life. In general, Daoism emphasizes harmony between man and nature, promoting the pursuit of governance without interference and a carefree life attitude.

Another very important school of Chinese philosophy is the philosophy of the mind (*Xinxue*) or Yangming theory, which was founded by Wang Yangming, a well-known philosopher in the Ming Dynasty. Yangming theory proposed several thoughts. Firstly, unity of knowledge and action, which emphasizes that human knowledge and behavior should be consistent, one's mind can be gradually developed and improved through the process of self-cultivation and practice, and only practical actions can prove whether an idea is correct or not. The second is studying the nature of things. In other words, only through the observation and thinking of the surrounding things, can one deeply understand the nature of things, find the shortcomings, and achieve self-improvement. The third is "mind is the reason." Yangming theory believes that the mind can transcend reality and experience; the mind is the essence of human intelligence and instinct, so only through internal harmony of reason and morality can one achieve the goal of life. The fourth thought is the "extension of intuitive knowledge," which emphasizes one's mindset and believes that only under the guidance of conscience can one achieve self-perfection and gain moral growth.

There are also other schools of thought. Mohism focuses on love and fairness, calling for non-aggression and universal love. Legalism emphasizes the rule of law and believes that law is the basis of governing the country, advocating the formulation of well-established laws, taking law as the standard of social behavior, and maintaining social order and fairness and justice through the regulation and implementation of law. Buddhism emphasizes that everything in the world has causes and results, the sentient beings need to know the nature, origin, and cessation of suffering and path, and practice the noble eightfold path to leave suffering and enjoy happiness.

The central focus of Chinese philosophy throughout the ages has been a practical concern with how to live an ideal life and how to organize a society. Ethics and political philosophy have often taken precedence over metaphysics and epistemology. Another characteristic of Chinese philosophy has been reflections on nature and the self, which have resulted in the development of themes like unity between man and heaven, the place of man in the cosmic order, and the explanations of differentiation and changes. Humanism has also been the chief attribute of Chinese philosophy. The role of human beings and their places in society have always been the main focus of Chinese thinkers. Practical, moral, and political concerns have been favored over metaphysical speculation as Chinese philosophy tends to be concerned with worldly affairs.

3.1.2 Western philosophy

Western philosophy originated in ancient Greece, where the soil was barren and the terrain was mountainous. As the land was unable to support an ever-increasing population, people had to turn to the sea for better opportunities. The development of navigation skills and the prosperity of trade directly and indirectly promoted cultural exchange. Advanced cultures from Egypt and Babylon continuously influenced Greece, where Eastern and Western ideas blended and collided, giving birth to the sprouting of Greek thoughts. The unique economic and geographical environment led Greeks to become people who "looked up at the stars," contemplating their relationship with the outside world. Since ancient Greece, Western philosophers have been devoted to contemplatig on the essence of the universe, human existence, and moral issues.

Socrates, perhaps the greatest philosophical personality in Greek history, has a profound influence on Western philosophy. He left no writings as records of his thoughts, but his teachings were preserved for later generations in the dialogues with his famous pupil Plato. Socrates taught that every person has full knowledge of the ultimate truth contained within the soul and needs only to be spurred to conscious reflection in order to become aware of it. A philosopher's task, Socrates believed, is to provoke people into thinking for themselves, rather than to teach them anything they did not already know. His contribution to the history of thought is not a systematic doctrine but a method of thinking and a way of life. He stressed the need for analytical examination of the grounds of one's beliefs, clear definitions of basic concepts, and a critical approach to ethical problems

Plato is the best-known Greek philosopher, whose metaphysical and epistemological thoughts have been influential in Western philosophy. One of his insights is the theory of ideas. To Plato, notions such as virtue, justice, beauty, and goodness, would not be possible unless one has some direct knowledge of these things in an earlier existence. One is born into this world with an imperfect memory of these forms. In the ideal world of ideas, one can experience the real forms which are perfect and universal. Our world is an imperfect parody of the Platonic flawless and superior world of ideas; knowledge of these forms is possible only through long and arduous study by philosophers but their eventual enlightenment would qualify them to rule the society.

Aristotle is one of the most profound and influential thinkers of the Western world. He defined many basic concepts and principles of the theoretical sciences such as logic, biology, physics, and psychology. In founding the science of logic, he developed the theory of deductive inference, represented by the syllogism and a set of rules for the scientific method. In his metaphysical theory, Aristotle criticized Plato's separation of form from matter and maintained that the forms or essences are contained within the concrete objects that exemplify them; everything real is a combination of potentiality and actuality.

Christianity also has a profound impact on Western philosophy. Medieval philosophers combined Christianity with philosophy and formed a unique worldview, defining the relationship between man and God.

Augustine emphasized the relationship between faith and reason. According to him, the earth is brought into existence from nothing by a perfectly good and just God, who created man. The earth is not eternal; the earth, as well as time, has both a beginning and an end. Man, on the other hand, is brought into existence to endure eternally. All men deserve damnation because of the Fall of Adam, as the result of which, all human beings are heirs to the effects of Adam's original sin, and all are vessels of pride, avarice, greed, and self-interest. Based on the concept, Augustine deemed justice the crucial distinction between ideal political states and non-ideal political states—the status of every political state on earth. According to him, there is no just state because men rejected the teachings of Christ.

Thomas Aquinas, an Italian Catholic priest in the early 13th century, has a profound influence on Western thoughts. As a controversial figure, he tried to explain theological problems through philosophy and explored the political theory of theology. He defended the feudal order and the authority of the church, and constructed a theological system including all sides through compromising standpoints of each school. According to him, the natural law is just like a bridge built between eternal law and human law. Eternal law is connected with ontology, divinity and stability, while natural law is basically one part of the eternal law inscribed on human nature by God. He pointed out that people have the right to resist tyranny, that law and power come from people, and that people should participate in politics. He proposed the freedom of thought, freedom of faith and freedom of spirit, and believed a country needs to implement the rule of law.

Descartes, a French philosopher and mathematician in the 17th century, ushered in a new era of modern philosophy through skepticism and rationalism. He proposed skepticism, believing that human knowledge is subject to delusion, illusion, and misdirection and that all beliefs and ideas should be questioned in order to pursue the certainty of truth. Based on self-consciousness, Descartes put forward the philosophical proposition of "I think, therefore I am." He believed that one's own existence can be determined through the process of thinking and doubting one's own existence. In the dualism of mind and matter, Descartes argued that the human body and the mind are different entities. He classified the human body and the natural world as the measurable material realm, and the human mind and consciousness as the immaterial spiritual realm. Descartes emphasized the importance of reason, believing that truth and knowledge could be obtained through pure rational thinking and reasoning. He advocated the use of mathematical and geometric methods to deduce philosophical problems in pursuit of certainty and universal knowledge.

John Locke was a British philosopher in the Age of Enlightenment in the 17th century. His thoughts have a profound effect on politics, education, epistemology, and other fields. His social contract theory argued that people live in a "state of nature" with innate equal rights, but in order to protect those rights, they voluntarily enter the social contract and create government; therefore, government derives its legitimacy from the consent of the people, and its powers should be limited to protect the life, liberty, and property of the people. He also proposed liberty and equality, believing that everyone is equal and has the right to life, liberty, and property, stressing that the government exists to guarantee these rights, not to violate or deny them. Locke emphasized the importance of private property rights, arguing that individuals acquire the ownership of natural resources by transforming them into property through labor. This idea has a profound impact on capitalist society and the legal system.

In addition to the abovementioned philosophers, many other philosophers also have contributed to the development of Western philosophy, such as Hegel, Nietzsche, Hume, Kant, Bacon, Marx, and so on.

3.2 Comparing the View of the World

View of the world, or world view, is also called the cosmological view, the general term for all space, time, and matter. It involves what kind of position we are in and what kind of time framework we use to look at and analyze things. It is the reaction of our judgment on things, the basic view and perspective of the world. Specifically, it is about who we are, where we come from, what is the world or universe around us, what significance they have for our survival, and how we should face life's thinking.

Different cultures inevitably have different world views, which are products of the thinking patterns and the ideological foundation of specific cultures. However, in turn, world views also greatly affect specific cultures and thinking patterns, shaping people's beliefs, values, emotions, and attitudes.

3.2.1 View of the world in Chinese philosophy

The world view of Chinese philosophy is a rich and complex subject, which has deep historical roots and unique cultural background. China is a mainland country with vast plains, distinct seasons, and well-developed agriculture. People were deeply concerned about the land, and government policies also prioritized land. Emphasizing agriculture over trade became the dominating economic policy in ancient China, and Chinese intellectuals also paid much attention to land and human centeredness, so Chinese thinking tended to "look down at the earth." Different from Western philosophy's contemplation of natural matters and the universe, Chinese philosophy focuses on humanistic ethics and morality. This does not mean that metaphysical ideas are absent from Chinese philosophy. An example of metaphysics in the Chinese tradition is the obscure document *The Book of*

Changes. Some Chinese take this book as a manual of divination. For those who can understand its messages, it is believed to contain all laws of nature.

The relationship between human beings and the world is the central concern in Chinese philosophy, which includes the use of wisdom in regard to human life, and various arguments regarding the perception of the world. The world view emphasizes the wholeness of the universe and the interactive relationship between man and nature, the harmony and balance among behavior, ration, and morality. Many classics, including *The Book of Changes*, discuss the relationship between nature and human beings. In the eyes of the traditional Chinese philosophers, people naturally have puzzles about life and the world, all derived from their misunderstanding of *dao*, the road one walks in life, which stands analogously to one's behavior and development. Throughout the journey, one remains unclear of his direction due to the lack of understanding of his own nature.

Classical thought, represented by Confucianism, holds that the order of the universe is established and maintained by limited and constantly changing groups (societies, nations, or families), and that individual happiness lies in learning the paths of these social groups. Confucianism also emphasizes a modest attitude toward the forces of nature, and the coordination of different forces and interests of different people, thus guiding people to achieve the greatest degree of co-prosperity and coexistence, so that the society can achieve long-term stability. Other philosophical thoughts, such as Daoism, Legalism, Buddhism, and so on, have different world views, but they also emphasize the ideas of harmony, balance, and common prosperity. Daoism, by following *dao*, non-action, non-action without interference, emphasizes observing the laws of nature through self-adjusting to achieve results that are beneficial to groups and individuals. Buddhism believes that all things in the world do not exist independently, nor are they eternal and invariable, but are produced by the interaction and cooperation of various causes and conditions. Therefore, nothing has a fixed self or essence in nature and is void. As a consequence, humans should follow the "four noble truths," and "eight noble paths" in order to plant good causes and good relationships, in order to lead a carefree life and know the real essence of life.

In Chinese philosophy, the subject and object, as well as the human and the external world, are in a harmonious and interconnected state. The uttermost pursuit is the spiritual realm of "unity between nature and man." As Confucius said, "Does the heaven say anything? The four seasons run, and all things grow. Does the heaven say anything?" Zhu Xi, a Neo-Confucianist, once said, "The laws of heaven and the laws of the human world are the same thing, and things in the human world and things in nature need to be integrated as one entity." These thoughts indicate that although our ancestors explored nature and searched for the laws of its operation, they did not pursue the underlying mechanism of the laws. Instead, they pursued the laws in order to live a better life, as the production mode of agriculture required them to master the laws of nature, but not to conquer nature. Consequently, the thinking mode of Chinese philosophy has emerged and gradually developed.

In Chinese epistemology, the subject and object are also in unity. People explore the natural laws in order to guide their activities. They follow the laws of nature, which are interconnected with the laws of man. Therefore, Chinese philosophy emphasizes the balance and change of *yin* and *yang*, believing that the world is composed of opposing but interdependent forces. The concept of unity expresses the close connection between humans and nature, as well as the interdependence between humans and society. A case in point is the *Daode Jing*, which advocates shaping the moral qualities of individuals and society in a non-coercive and non-confrontational manner. In addition, Chinese philosophy emphasizes the importance of harmony and balance, maintaining a harmonious relationship between individuals and society, as well as between humans and nature. Nature is regarded as an organic whole, and humans should maintain harmonious coexistence with nature.

This epistemology attaches importance to wholeness, comprehensiveness, and adaptability, emphasizing harmonious coexistence with the environment and adherence to natural laws. To actively integrate man with nature, it is necessary to ponder the reasons from multiple aspects, and unify them to form a whole and consider them comprehensively. This is how the world view shapes the Chinese way of thinking. We tend to look at things from a holistic, dialectal perspective, with a moderate approach, and try to find a balance point that can do things well, making ourselves and others satisfied.

Chinese philosophy pays much attention to dialectical thinking. Since Laozi and Confucius, many Chinese thinkers have advocated dialectical thinking, empathizing with the unity of opposites, especially the unity and harmony, and proposed that the integration of harmony and the opposites is the most important.

3.2.1 View of the world in Western philosophy

Western philosophy has a different cosmology and epistemology from the Chinese. Since ancient Greece, Western people have had a high level of cognitive enthusiasm, considering seeking knowledge and reflecting on the matters in the universe as the pleasures of life. Socrates believed that contemplation was a symbol of perfection and nobility in the human soul. He often advised Athenian citizens not to pursue fame and fortune with all their might, while ignoring knowledge, truth, and the beauty of the soul. According to him, a life without thought was worthless, and a valuable life was one that never stopped seeking knowledge and philosophical contemplation. The speculative spirit of ancient Greece not only shaped the tradition of critical thinking in Western philosophy but also gave birth to the spirit of Western science. Science, in turn, has influenced the development of philosophy.

Western philosophy and science share the same cosmology and epistemology, namely, binary opposition. The most classic example of binary opposition is the dichotomy between rational and emotional, between presence and absence. Other examples include male as opposed to female, speech as opposed to writing, and so on. "I think, therefore I am" is a very typical explanation of binary opposition, which emphasizes individual thinking. It deems human thinking as the scale of nature, and puts humans in opposition to nature. In Greek mythology, there exist both man's worship of gods and the imperfect nature of gods, who also have human flaws. These stories exhibit both worship and contempt, desire and rationality, which are opposite. The theology of the Medieval Ages was the authority of various disciplines, but many scientists constantly broke the shackles of religion, and promoted the development of science. These opposing categories reflect the Western way of understanding things, from the inside to the outside, from the surface to the inside, acknowledging the differences, respecting individual thoughts, and ultimately developing into the pursuit of freedom and equality, which is the foundation of democracy.

As the world view is closely related to the way of thinking, in Western philosophy, rationality has always received higher evaluations than sensibility. Western philosophy emphasizes logical and analytical thinking, rationality and logic, seeking truth and wisdom through speculation and analysis, clarifying concepts, exploring relationships, and solving problems with analytical thinking. From ancient Greece to modern times, especially in modern Western philosophy, analytical methods are very popular. After the 16th century, metaphysical thinking emerged, which regarded things as isolated and static.

3.3 Comparing View of Knowledge and Truth

The view of knowledge refers to how to understand knowledge and what attitude one holds toward knowledge, which affects the learning and teaching process, and a learner's view on knowledge and learning is the innate mechanism of the learning activities. The view of truth refers to the standard of truth that a learner believes in when he learns and seeks knowledge. It determines the true or false judgment and belief selection of "ideas/knowledge." Concerning the view of knowledge and truth, there exist two philosophical schools, materialism and idealism.

Materialism has a long history. It has gone through three historical forms or stages, namely, ancient naive materialism, modern metaphysical materialism, and modern dialectical materialism. In the tortuous course of human beings moving from ignorance to civilization, it has played an important and positive role. Materialism has two cores: matter and consciousness; it also has two laws: monism (the principle of the unity of matter in the world), and the principle of the dialectical relationship between matter and consciousness. Materialism believes that consciousness is the product of the long-term development of the material world (nature and society), the subjective reflection of the objective world, an approximate and active reflection of the objective existence; any consciousness is a projection of the objective existence, based on the prototype from the objective existence. The content of consciousness is objective and its form is subjective. Consciousness is the organic unity of objective content and subjective form.

Idealism holds that subjective consciousness is the primary quality of the world and matter is the secondary. It absolutizes certain links or stages of the process of cognition, exaggerates the role of subjective consciousness, and abstracts subjective consciousness into "entities" that dominate everything other than human beings, so that the subjective and material world are inverted. The two subtypes, subjective idealism, and objective idealism, have their different theories.

Subjective idealism regards the subjective consciousness of the subject, such as feeling, experience, mind, idea, will, and so on, as the source and basis of the emergence and existence of all things in the conscious world, while all things in the external world are derived from the subjective consciousness, and are the manifestations of the subjective consciousness. Thus, in the view of subjective idealists, the subjective consciousness is primary, while the things of the external world are derived and secondary. Subjective idealism regards everything in the external world as the manifestation and product of the subjective consciousness of the self, and everything in the external world is determined by the subjective consciousness. As a consequence, without the subjective consciousness, there will be no things in the external world; that is, the existence of the objective world depends on the subjective consciousness.

Objective idealism points out that objective consciousness is a reality that exists before and is independent of the material world, while the material world (or external world) is the externalization or expression of the objective consciousness; the former is original and primary, while the latter is derivative and secondary. Objective consciousness is the result of absolutizing human thoughts or general concepts, sublimating or distilling them through abstract thinking into entities that exist independently not only of the human mind but also of or before the material world and concrete things, and further deifying and idolizing them. Therefore, objective idealism and religion are often closely related: objective idealism is a more refined form of religion, while religion is an ideal form of objective idealism.

3.3.1 View of knowledge and truth in Chinese philosophy

In Chinese philosophy, there are both materialism and idealism, both having abundant thinkers and theories. In the Shang Dynasty (1600–1046 BCE), Chinese people still worshiped and acted on the divination of ghosts and gods. But the following dynasty, the Western Zhou Dynasty, broke the superstition of divination based on ghosts and gods, and the element of materialism gradually emerged ever since, including the "yin-yang" theory, "five elements" theory, "qi" theory, and so on, which indicated the unity and changing law of the universe and nature.

The "yin-yang" theory holds that the world is a material entirety, everything in nature includes the two opposing aspects of *yin* and *yang*, and the opposing sides are unified with each other. The movement of the unity of opposites between *yin* and *yang* is the fundamental cause of the occurrence, development, change, and extinction of all things in nature. The "yin-yang" theory believes that everything in the world contains the unity of opposites, which refer to two opposing forces, factors, trends, positions, and so on. They are opposite to each other but unified. The "five elements" theory holds that wood, fire, earth, metal, and water are the most essential substances that constitute the material world, and the material world is formed because of the mutual support and restriction among these substances. It emphasizes that there is a connection among the movement of the five substances, and that there are generating and overcoming cycles among them. The five elements are not only regarded as the origin of the world but also used to explain the connection and development of the world through the relationship among them. The "yin-yang" and "five elements" theories were integrated into one philosophical system in the Warring States period.

Ancient Chinese materialists believed that all things in the universe are composed of a very subtle flowing material "*qi*," which is the origin of the world, and put forward the theory of *qi* monism, believing that the material and unified *qi* constitute all things in nature, and man is a part of nature, "Nature and earth are *qi*; all things are born by themselves," "The matter cannot exist without *qi*, and *qi* gathers to form all matters." These are the simple reflections of the materialist thought that matter is primary and consciousness is secondary.

There is also idealism, such as the philosophy of the mind, which advocated that "mind is reason," "The universe is my mind, and my mind is the universe," believing that to understand the universe as it is, one must know his mind, and opposed the pursuit of "the maximum truth" and "study the nature of things," because the truth is endless, to study the nature of things is too tiring, so one should find out the "reason" from his own mind, because "reason" lies in the human mind and transforms into all things in the universe.

Whatever materialism or idealism, Chinese philosophy emphasizes the concept of unity of knowledge and action, and believes that the combination of knowledge and practice is the key to the true functioning of knowledge. The true meaning of knowledge lies in transforming it into action and experience through practice. Chinese philosophy also values the application of theory to practice, verifying and improving knowledge through practice, making it of practical guiding significance.

Chinese philosophy also values individual experience and intuition, believing that understanding the world through one's own experience and intuition is an important source of knowledge. Experience is seen as an intuitive and direct way to acquire knowledge, and through perception and personal experience, one can gain a profound understanding of specific contexts. Individual intuition is considered a manifestation of comprehension and insight, through which one can capture the essence and internal connections of things.

3.3.2 View of knowledge and truth in Western philosophy

There are numerous representative materialists and idealists in the West. Descartes put forward the idea of "universal doubt." His philosophical ideas of rationalism deeply influenced subsequent generations of Europeans and laid the foundation for rationalist philosophy in Europe. One of his best quoted sayings is "I think, therefore I am." He believed that humans should be able to use mathematical methods and reason, to think philosophically. He discovered four rules from logic, geometry, and algebra. The first is, whatever one does not clearly recognize, he will never accept it as true. In other words, one should be careful to avoid hasty judgments and preconceptions, and to put nothing else into his judgment than what is so clearly present in his mind that he cannot doubt it at all. The second is to divide each difficult question one examines into parts so that it might be properly solved. The third is, to think in order, beginning with the simplest and most recognizable objects, until the most complex objects are known. The fourth rule is, in any case, one should try to investigate as comprehensively and widely as possible to make sure that nothing is missed. Reason, he believed, is more reliable than the senses.

Rationalism has played an important role in Western philosophy, which emphasizes the application of rationality and logic, emphasizing the acquisition of knowledge through reasoning and analysis. Rationality is seen as an important cognitive tool that can help man think and understand the essence of the world. By applying the rules and principles of logical thinking, one can engage in rigorous thinking and deduction, thus forming reasonable conclusions.

Positivism as one branch of rationalism, also has a profound impact on Western philosophy. It emphasizes the establishment of truth through observation, empirical evidence, and empirical verification. Empirical science stresses the importance of empirical methods, and experimental verification, and the acquisition of knowledge through observation and evidence.

Empiricism is opposed to rationalism. It holds that perceptual experience is the source of knowledge, and all knowledge is acquired through experience and verified in experience, just as Locke denied the concept of talent and believed that "*all our knowledge is based on experience and comes from experience in the final analysis.*" He believed that the mind is like a blank slate, and all knowledge comes from the perceptual experience obtained by observing things. The mind also has a sense of distinction, comparison, and generalization of sensory impressions.

3.4 Chapter Summary

Chinese philosophy is influenced by schools of thought such as *The Book of Changes*, Confucianism, Taoism, Mohism, Buddhism, and so on, which tends to "look down at the earth," exploring the worldly things. Western philosophy originated from ancient Greek philosophy and has been heavily influenced by Christianity, medieval philosophy, the Renaissance, and Enlightenment, which tends to "look up at the sky," contemplating the unworldly things.

There is a great difference between Chinese and Western philosophy in their approach to the fundamental issues of the world. The world view of Chinese philosophy emphasizes the harmony of *yin* and *yang*, the unity of nature and man, and the dialectical thinking mode centered on harmony, balance, and nature, Chinese people view the world from the perspective of the unity of nature and man, while the world view in Western philosophy is reflected by binary opposition and the emphasis on logical and analytical thinking, perceiving the world from the perspective of binary opposition.

The ethics of Chinese philosophy emphasize the values of benevolence, filial piety, and social harmony, and advocate the power of morality. The political value of Chinese philosophy emphasizes absolute monarchy and the Confucian concept of governance. It is the monarch's responsibility to rule by virtue to ensure social harmony and order. Chinese philosophy also values the importance of hierarchy and etiquette in regulating social relationships and ways of behavior. On the other hand, Western philosophy focuses on individual rights and utilitarianism, applied ethics and ethical relativism. In addition, the political value of Western philosophy emphasizes the concepts of democracy and social contracts, believing that political power should come from the participation and consent of the people. The pursuit of individual rights and social justice is also an important political value, emphasizing individual freedom and the fair distribution of social resources.

In both Chinese and Western philosophy, there are materialist and idealist thoughts. Chinese philosophy emphasizes the importance of integrating knowledge and action with practice, and the combination of theory with practice. It values individual experience and intuition, believing that through direct observation and experience, one can better understand the world. On the other hand, Western philosophy is based on science, emphasizing the application of rationality and logic, emphasizing the acquisition of knowledge and truth through reasoning and analysis.

Meanwhile, it also values positivist and empirical science, stressing the importance of positivity and falsifiability, objectivity and universality.

As products of human civilization and wisdom, Chinese and Western philosophy also share similarities. Firstly, they both demonstrate humanistic care, focus on human life and happiness, emphasize the relationship between people, and pursue social harmony and justice. Secondly, both are exploration of knowledge, committed to understanding the world. Although there are differences in the view of how to acquire knowledge and truth, both emphasize speculation, the pursuit of wisdom, and the exploration of the meaning of human existence. Thirdly, both have made significant contributions to the development of human civilization. They have unique contributions and values, playing important roles in the development and inheritance of Eastern and Western civilizations.

Comparing Chinese and Western philosophy promotes a more comprehensive understanding of human mindset and cultural development. Firstly, the value of mutual learning lies in engaging in dialogues and communication. By comparison and contrast, it is possible to enhance mutual understanding and respect. Secondly, it is possible to inherit and innovate knowledge. Absorbing the essence of the two philosophies can help develop more intelligent ways of thinking and problem-solving methods, and provide more effective guidance for the contemporary society. Thirdly, it helps to explore common values. Despite the differences, Chinese and Western philosophy share many common values, such as caring for others, and pursuing justice and equality. Through communication and dialogue, we can explore these common values and work together to build a more harmonious, just, and prosperous world.

3.5 Case Study Assignments

Assignment 3-1 Please read the excerpt below and answer the questions.

> Of the three main flows of philosophical thought, it has been maintained that the Indian is otherworldly, the Greek unworldly, and the Chinese worldly. No philosophy is ever plainly worldly; to say that it is so merely an attempt to caricature it in order to bring out certain features into striking relief. To those who know something of Chinese philosophy the word "worldly" merely emphasizes certain

features in comparison with the Indian and the Greek school of thought; but to those who do not know anything about it, that word is liable to be quite misleading. What is meant is probably that Chinese philosophy sticks to the kernel of its subject matter; it is never propelled by the instruments of things either into the dizzy heights of systematic speculation, or into the depth of a labyrinth of elaborate barrenness. Like machines in industrial civilization, intellectuality in philosophy drives; and whether it drives us into blind alleys or not, it may lead us far away from the wide boulevards or spacious squares. Intellectually, Chinese philosophy has always been in the open air.

We are accustomed to thinking of Chinese philosophy as consisting of Confucianism, Buddhism, and Taoism. It is rather as religious that these are exclusively mentioned, etc. In the early stages both Confucianism and Taoism were only philosophies, and as such they were in the pre-Qin period members of a whole democracy of different schools of thought, the variety of which during that period was unparalleled in Chinese history. Since terms are inadequate, we shall refrain from any attempt at description. It is misleading enough to apply the familiar philosophical terms to Western philosophy, it is much worse to apply them to the Chinese. One might say for instance that there were logicians in the pre-Qin period; but if so, readers might be led to think that there were people who brooded over syllogism, or the laws of thought, or even obversion and conversion. The Yin-Yang-ists have been described in a recent article as the precursors of science, and now without foundation either, but then they were precursors of something which strictly speaking never arrived; and if as a result of this description readers imagine them to be ancient Keplers or Galileos, they entertain a distorted view of a while brand of thinkers.

Confucianism and Taoism are indigenous to China, they are properly Chinese; Buddhism, however, was introduced from India and it might be wondered whether it could be said to be Chinese. The introduction of a foreign philosophy is not quite the same as the importance of foreign goods. In the last century, for instance, the English were alarmed at the invasion of German Idealism. *"The Rhine,"* they declared, *"has flowed into the Thames."* But however alarmed they might be, their Thames has not since become a mere Rhine; British Hegelianism while acknowledging its origin and impetus from abroad is distinctly English, though it is not so characteristically English as the philosophies of Locke and Hume. Buddhism in China, in the early stages, at any rate, had been modified by Chinese thought: indeed for a time, it was robed in Taoist garbs and Taoism, it might be said, became its chief agency of distribution. But there was something stubborn in Buddhism which resisted Taoistic manipulations, hence although it became Chinese to some extent, it is not distinguished by the features characteristic of the indigenous Chinese philosophy.

(Jin, 2019, pp. 2-3)

Questions:

(1) Do you agree with the idea that "Greek philosophy is unworldly and the Chinese philosophy is worldly"? Why or why not?

(2) Do you think it is misleading to apply the familiar philosophical terms of Chinese philosophy to Western philosophy, or explain Chinese philosophy with terms of Western philosophy? Why or why not?

(3) How do you view the introduction of foreign philosophy into Chinese philosophy, or in a broader view, the integration of philosophy from different cultures?

Assignment 3-2 Please read the following passage and answer questions.

儒教之以人为中心而观天地万物与西方哲学的目的观、意匠观相似，而《列子·说符》篇有一"超卓之见解"则与近代进化论思想相通。《说符》篇云："天地万物与我并生，类也。类无贵贱。徒以大小智力而相制，迭相食，非相为而生之。"王国维认为，这段话"与近世所谓弱肉强食，生存竞争，优胜劣汰，即生物进化论之思想，隐隐相通。……此种思想以较儒教之以人为中心，而观天地万物者，又基督教之一派或西洋哲学之一派之目的观、意匠观……固不失为别开生面之见地矣。"由此可见，中西哲学在天人关系方面皆有以人为中心的目的观和意匠观相反的看法。当然，此类论述并不只是《列子》中才有，尚可于其他典籍中见之，如王廷相《慎言》《雅述》中的相关论述足以与上引《列子·说符》之说相参证。

(Xu, 2009, p27)

Questions:

(1) How do you explain the idea that there are similarities between Chinese and Western philosophy?

(2) In addition to the similarities mentioned in the above passage, what are the other similarities?

References

Feng, Y. L. (1996). *Zhongguo zhexue jianshi* [*A brief history of Chinese philosophy*] (2nd ed.). Peking University Press.

Feng, Y. L. (1996). *Sansongtang quanji* [*The complete works of sansongtang*]. Henan People's Press.

Jin, Y. L. (2019). *Dao, ziran yu ren* [*Dao, nature and man*]. Foreign Language Teaching and Research Press.

Jin Y. L. (1995). *Jin Yuelin wenji* [*The collected works of Jin Yuelin*]. Gansu People's Press.

Hu, S. (1998). *Hu Shi wenji.* [*The collected works of Hu Shi*]. Peking University Press.

Wang, Y., & Zhao, M. D. (2017). *Zhongxi wenhua bijiao* [*The comparison between Chinese and Western culture*]. Tsinghua University Press.

Xu, S. M. (2009). Lun Wang Guowei de zhongxi zhexue bijiao yanjiu: pushi zhexue dingyi guanzhao xia de zhongxi huijing [On Wang Guowei's comparative study of Chinese and Western philosophies: Chinese and Western philosophical wisdom from the perspective of universal hilosophy]. *Chinese Philosophy, 9*:29-32,128.

Thilly, F (2015). *A History of Philosophy*. Peking University Press.

Wen, H., M., (2020). *Chinese Philosophy*. Chinese International Press.

Comparing Values

Tian Mei

Chapter One has introduced the definitions, features, and functions of culture. Values are important components of the non-material, invisible culture. Growing up in a culture, people gradually internalize social values which in turn influence what they think and how they act. This chapter focuses on values. It first introduces definitions of values. It then focuses on Chinese and Western values as observed in everyday life and summarized in teaching materials on cross-cultural communication.

Values are the focuses of empirical research in the field of cross-cultural studies. For example, in the 1970s and 1980s, less than 8% of the articles published in the *Journal of Cross-Cultural Psychology* (JCCP) focused on values. In the years 2007 to 2009, over 20% of the JCCP articles stressed values, indicating the centrality of values in cross-cultural studies (Knafo, Roccas & Sagiv, 2011). For this reason, this chapter also reviews research findings on values, in particular, Hofstede's survey studies and the value dimensions that he developed based on his survey findings. The chapter ends with a discussion on the reviewed literature and an application of what has been discussed.

4.1 Definitions of Values

Schwartz (2006, p.139) defined values as "*the cultural ideals*". They are the collective understandings of what is good, correct, desirable, and proper in a given culture. Values regulate our daily behaviors, guiding us to "*select actions, evaluate people and events, and explain their actions and evaluations*" (Schwartz, 1999, pp.23–47). Regarded as the most important feature of culture, values "*promote coherence among the various aspects of culture*" (*ibid*). Within a society, values function to form a collective identity, integrating, uniting, and binding social members together.

In Chapter One, we discussed the characteristics of culture. As an important cultural element, values share similar features with culture. First, values are learned within a cultural context (Samovar, Porter & McDaniel, 2012). Different from personal goals which are related to specific situations, values are broad, general social goals which apply to various situations (Sagiv, Sverdlik & Schwarz, 2011).

Second, values are "*transmitted by a variety of sources*" (Samovar, Porter & McDaniel, 2012, p.138). Inherently desirable, values are communicated and shared among social members (Sagiv, Sverdlik & Schwarz, 2011). Third, values affect how members of a society interpret the social world and how they act accordingly. They serve as standards and criteria, " ... *tell* [ing] *people what is normal by identifying what things are good and bad, or right and wrong*" (Samovar, Porter & McDaniel, 2012, pp.138–139).

In addition, values are not "*intrinsic and universal*", but rather socially constructed in space and time (Avrami et al., 2000, see Stephenson, 2008, p.129). For social members, different values bear with them different importance, forming a subjectively perceived hierarchical value system (Sagiv, Sverdlik & Schwarz, 2011).

4.2 Reflective Observation

4.2.1 Researching Chinese values

Much research has focused on cultural values. For example, researchers have referred to Confucius' teaching, particularly the significance of interpersonal relationships, as the key to their interpretation of Chinese values. Here the interpersonal relationships refer to the five fundamental hierarchical relationships, i.e. the relationship between husband and wife, between emperor and officials, between father and son, between elder and younger brothers, and between elder and younger friends. The researchers, based on Confucius' teaching, stress the following important Chinese values, i.e. compassion for others and respect for righteous actions, which are intended to facilitate good social relationships.

One prolific researcher studying Chinese values is D. Y. F. Ho, who has written numerously on social relation, or *guanxi* in Chinese, person-in-relation, and relational identity. Starting from the five cardinal relationships, her work stresses interdependence, or interrelatedness, as the essential value of a Confucian society. By proposing "methodological relationalism", Ho (1998) argues that in the Confucian culture, individual behaviours are strongly influenced by their social concerns, and that the standards that individuals follow to conduct appropriate actions are not self-perception, preference or personal needs, but the attitudes, obligations or indebtedness of related others. In other words, according to this researcher, individual identity is formed upon the social relations and the characters of the groups he/she belongs to in a Confucian society. Since everyone shares the attributes of a particular group and the society as a whole, they benefit from the increase but suffer from the decrease of the group's social reputation.

Other researchers, such as Bloom and Solokto (2003), have studied compassion, another important Confucian value. According to their interpretation, the concept of compassion is an umbrella term for virtues, with love as the underlying principle. They argue that compassion reflects Confucius' firm belief that a ruler should govern his subjects by moral power and should treat them with virtue, love, and concern so as to win their hearts without resorting to physical force (Bloom & Solokto, 2003). Bloom and Solokto (2003) also point out that compassion continues to play a crucial role in modern societies that functions to maintain harmonious social relations.

Similarly, it is well documented that Confucian filial piety acts to regulate Chinese people's behaviours with respect to intergenerational relationships, which concern not only the relationship between child and parents but also the relationship between descendants and ancestors (see Bloom & Solokto, 2003; Ho, 1998). According to Sung (1998), the core of filial piety is affection but unconditional submission. It involves a set of strict requirements which one has to follow from birth to death (*ibid*). For example, one holds the responsibilities of caring for one's aged parents and meeting both their emotional and material needs. It has been argued that filial piety harmonizes the relationships in their family, which in turn harmonize the society (Bloom & Solokto, 2003).

K. Hwang is a prolific social psychologist. He has published numerously on social favour, or *renqing* in Chinese, stressing that *renqing*, closely related to interpersonal relationships, is another cultural value featuring Chinese society. In an article entitled "Face and favour: the Chinese power game" (1987), he refers to the concept of *renqing* as a set of hidden rules or social norms regulating individuals' behaviours in Chinese society. Briefly, within diverse social groups, every member should keep emotionally in touch with others; whoever confronts difficulties should be given a hand; and those who have been given a favour should be grateful and try their best to help others in return. Since all people, following the standards of social exchange, try to get along well with others and manage their social network well, *renqing* functions to bind together social members and contributes to the integration of Chinese society.

In the same article, Hwang (1987) points out the significance of "face" or *mianzi* in Chinese. For him, *mianzi* plays a similarly crucial role with *renqing* and *guanxi* in maintaining a harmonious Chinese society. He emphasizes two types of "face-work", both of which consist of a set of strategies including face-saving, face-gaining, face-giving, and avoiding loss of face. Specifically, one type is the so-called horizontal face-work. The horizontal face-work means that face position could be increased by a person's intellectual attainment, increasing wealth and moral reputation. It can also be enhanced through one's connection with others belonging to a higher social class and through actions beneficial to society.

The vertical face-work, by contrast, refers to how individuals manipulate and project a favourable self-image in order to gain benefit from other people maximally. For example, in Leung and Chan's research (2003, p.1593), Hong Kong negotiators were found to engage in face-work to "*seek competitive advantages in a complex Chinese society*".

Differently from Hwang, in another article, Ho, Fu, and Ng (2004) clarify two dimensions of "face". Hwang only works on *mianzi*. Ho works on *lian* and *mianzi*. According to Ho, *lian* concerns the characters of a decent and morally good person, while *mianzi* refers to the reputation and social status achieved through one's efforts. Particularly, Ho and his colleagues stress the emotional significance of losing face. According to the authors, people may experience unbearable sufferings from their inability to act in a socially acceptable way, to perform in accordance with their social status, and to achieve socially expected ends. The loss of face could involve damage of confidence, severe self-criticism, and isolation from relatives and intimate friends. The loss of face can also be accompanied by feelings of anxiety, depression, shame, and guilt. Therefore, although enhancement of face always brings the acquisition of individual prestige and glorification of the whole family, avoiding losing face is the primary concern for Chinese people.

The researchers mentioned above have emphasized that Confucian values are not only related to traditional Chinese society but also remain important in modern Confucian-culture societies. A similar observation has been given by P. Burger in his edited book *In Search of an East Asian Model*, for example, stresses the significance of *Confucian-derived values* in explaining East Asian countries' economic success. As he argued,

> ... the development of modernity in the West suggests a reciprocal relationship with individualism ... The East Asian experience ... makes this assumption less self-evident ... Confucianism is a very powerful force ... explaining the economic performance of these [East Asian] countries ... (Berger, 1988, pp.6-7).

4.2.2 Hofstede's value dimensions

Among the empirical research on cultural values, one of the earliest attempts is the quantitative surveys conducted by Hofstede. Hofstede (1980) has investigated multi-national management in IBM branches in over 50 countries. Based on the research findings, Hofstede explains cultural value differences in terms of four dimensions—individualism/collectivism, power distance, uncertainty avoidance, and masculinity/femininity—and in his 1991 work, he proposed a fifth dimension, long- and short-term orientation. The Confucian emphasis on relationships is evident in Hofstede's work, which characterizes Chinese culture by its collectivism and high power distance (*ibid*). The following section will first introduce Hofstede's dimensions of power distance and individualism/collectivism before moving on to long- and short-term orientation.

Power-distance-index dimension

Specifically, the power-distance-index dimension expresses the degree to which "*the less powerful members of a society accept or expect that power is distributed unequally*" (Hofstede, 2010, p.61). The most crucial issue is about how a society handles the inequality among social members. In a society featured by high power distance, social members accept a hierarchical social order and the inequality of power. In a society featured by low power distance, social members strive to equalize the distribution of power and demand explanation for the inequality of social power.

Hofstede (2011) has provided key features of high power-distance societies in contrast to those of low power-distance societies. To be specific, in a high-power distance society, inequality is considered normal. People with power decide what is right and what is wrong. Children are taught to show respect to people having superior positions. To show respect is regarded as an important moral virtue. Education is teacher-centered. Subordinates do what they are told, and uneven income inequality exists. By contrast, in a low-power distance society, power is restricted. Children are treated by parents as equals. Education is student-centered. Subordinates are involved in the decision-making process. Income distribution is rather even.

Hofstede (2010) measures a society's power-distance-index (PDI) value using a scale ranging from zero to a hundred points. A value of near-zero stands for the smallest power distance, and a value of near a hundred points stands for the largest power distance. Here are some countries' PDI values, as adapted from Hofstede (2010, pp.57–59, see Table 4.1). From the table, we can see that high-power distance societies tend to be non-English speaking, developing countries, such as Russia and Mexico, while low-power distance societies tend to be English speaking, developed Western societies, such as the United States, Netherlands, Australia, Germany, Britain, and Denmark.

Table 4.1 Power distance index (PDI)

High PDI		Low PDI	
Index	Country	Index	Country
104	Malaysia	50	Italy
93	Russia	40	United States
78	Indonesia	39	Canada
77	India	38	Australia
74	Singapore	35	Germany
54	Japan	35	Great Britain
		18	Denmark

Individualism/collectivism dimension

Individualism/collectivism is another cultural dimension proposed by Hofstede to describe value differences between national societies. Individualism refers to a society characterized by weak ties between individuals, in which the individuals are expected to be responsible for themselves or close relatives only (Hofstede, 2010). Collectivism refers to a society characterized by strong ties between social members, who " ... *are integrated into strong, cohesive in-groups ...* " (Hofstede, 2010, p.92).

Hofstede (2011) has clarified the features of individualist and collectivist societies. According to him, in a collectivist society, interpersonal relationships are important. A person's social identity is emphasized.

People are classified as in- or out-group members. Social harmony is regarded as important. Education is to learn how to do. Moreover, building and maintaining interpersonal relationships are more important than the completion of a task. By contrast, in an individualist society, individual identities rather than social relationships are emphasized. People are classified as individuals. Individual actualization is more important than the maintenance of social harmony. Education is to learn how to learn. Completing a task is more important than maintaining social relationships.

According to Hofstede (2010), a society's individualist value could be measured on a scale from zero point to 100 points. A score close to zero stands for the most collectivist and a score close to 100 stands for the most individualist society. From Table 4.2 (see also Hofstede, 2010, pp.95–97), we can see the Western countries such as the United States, Australia, and Britain have high individualist scores and are individualist countries, while Japan, Russia, and Malaysia have low individualist scores and are collectivist countries.

Table 4.2 Individualism (IDV) index

High IDV		Low IDV	
Index	Country	Index	Country
91	United States	46	Japan
90	Australia	39	Russia
89	Great Britain	30	Mexico
80	Canada	26	Malaysia
80	Netherlands	20	Singapore
79	New Zealand	18	Republic of Korea
74	Denmark		

Long- and short-term orientation

In his work published in 1991, Hofstede proposed the fifth value dimension, i.e. the long- and short-term orientation. The fifth dimension is also known as "Confucian dynamism", indicating that the proposal of the dimension has drawn on the Confucius' ideas. According to Hofstede and Bond (1988, p.16), the positive pole of the dimension "*reflects a dynamic, future-oriented mentality, whereas its negative pole reflects a more static, tradition-oriented mentality*". As specified in Hofstede (2011), the long-term orientation is featured by persistence, ordering relationships by status, thrift, and having a sense of shame. In contrast, the short-term orientation is featured by avoidance of changes, stresses on face, respect for tradition, and reciprocation of greetings, favors and gifts.

According to Hofstede (2011), in a long-term oriented society, the future is important. The superior should adapt to the circumstances. The good and the bad are relative. Rules are not rigid, and traditions can be changed. People are expected to be humble. Students attribute success to efforts. Countries should learn from other countries and show fast economic growth. By contrast, in a short-term oriented society, the past and the present are important. The superior never adapts. The good and the bad are considered absolute. Rules and norms are fixed. Traditions cannot be changed. People should be proud of themselves and proud of their own countries. Students attribute success to luck. Countries show slow or no economic growth.

As shown in Table 4.5 (see also Hofstede, 2010, p.240), a country's Confucian dynamism, or its long-term oriented value, has been measured on a scale from zero to 100 points. A score close to zero stands for a short-term orientation, while a score close to one hundred stands for a long-term orientation. Brazil, Japan and Republic of Korea are the long-term oriented. This long-term orientation value has been drawn on by Hofstede to explain East Asian societies' dramatic economic growth since the 1980s.

Table 4.3 Long-term orientation (LTO) index

High LTO		Low LTO	
Index	Country	Index	Country
80	Japan	33	Sweden
75	Republic of Korea	31	Australia
65	Brazil	31	Germany
61	India	30	New Zealand
56	Thailand	29	United States
48	Singapore	25	Great Britain
		23	Canada

4.3 Abstract Conceptualization: Stereotyping and Stereotypes

Activity 4-1 How would you evaluate Hofstede's work on cultural values of different countries?

Insightful as it is, Hofstede's work is not free from problems. This section introduces the concepts of stereotyping and stereotypes, which will help to further discuss Hofstede's value dimensions in Section 4.5.

Stereotyping is cognitive processes which categorize social groups, social behaviors and social phenomena into fixed groups. While inevitably we draw on categories to understand and interpret the social world, stereotyping is dangerous as it focuses on a limited number of unchangeable features, freezing social groups and social phenomena in time and space, and ignoring many possible differences (O'sullivan et al., 1994).

Stereotypes are over-simplified, over-generalized labels imposed on social groups and social phenomena which are diverse and complex in nature. Value stereotypes are fixed, exaggerated beliefs attributed to the members of a social group. There exist two types of value stereotypes. The auto-stereotypes relate to the fixed and over-generalized beliefs of members of a social group about their own attributes. In contrast, the hetero-stereotypes relate to fixed and over-generalized beliefs about the attributes of other social groups (Dobewall & Strack, 2011). Stereotypes, which compare beliefs of other social groups against those of one's own, serve to distinguish in-groups and out-groups (*ibid*). In nature, value stereotypes are judgments and can easily turn into bias and prejudice (Holliday, 2004).

4.4 Active Experimentation: Re-thinking Hofstede's Value Dimensions

Hofstede's work has been widely challenged. His fifth dimension of cultural dynamism, for example, is questioned by Fang (2003; 2005). According to Fang (2003; 2005), the fifth dimension mistakenly divides the interrelated cultural values into opposing poles; the dimension ignores the fact that historical orientations such as respect for ancestors are also an articulated core value for Chinese people. Besides, Fang (2003; 2005) questions the fifth dimension as being based on methodologically weak research, in terms of using unrepresentative samples and misinterpretation in translations, and hence, lacking validity.

Moreover, the dialectical approach introduced in Chapter One stresses that, despite the crucial significance of values in forming social norms and creating a society in solidarity, the stereotypical descriptions of cultural values are dangerous. Hofstede's value dimensions, for example, can be criticized as overgeneralization, and over-simplification which demarcate (see Section

1.5.3), overlooking internal differences and possible changes of values over time. The common values of all mankind will be introduced in Section 4.6.

Another problem of Hofstede's value dimensions is that they tend to construct positive stereotypes of the "*quintessential American* [Western] *values*" (Sullivan, 2000, as cited in Holliday, 2005, p.20) in contrast to the negative stereotypes of "*somewhat backward*" non-Western values (see Holliday, 2005, p.20). Holliday (2004; 2005, p.20) has taught us how "*problematic*" images of the East are projected as the cultural *Other* against the "*unproblematic self*" of the West. The depictions, as listed in Table 4.6, reveal the connection among cultural stereotypes, ethnocentric, and Eurocentric.

Table 4.4 Images of the cultural *Other*

Unproblematic *Self*	Culturally Problematic *Other*
"Native speaker	"Non-native speaker
Independent, autonomous, creative, original	Dependent, hierarchical, collectivist, reticent Passive, docile, lacking in self-esteem
Individualist	Reluctant to challenge authority, easily dominated
Respecting privacy, choice, equality, freedom, change	Traditional, Confucian, etc. Uncritical, static, rigid, good at memorizing
Modern, Western	
Analytical, objective, flexible, critical, negotiating knowledge	Need to be trained, treated sensitively, understood, involved, given ownership, empowered"
Able to manage, research, plan, evaluate, make decisions"	(Holliday, 2005, p.20)

4.5 Common Values of Humanity[1]

In September 2015, during the general debate of the 70th session of the United Nations General Asssembly, Chinese President Xi Jinping proposed that "*Peace, development, equity, justice, democracy, and freedom are common values of all mankind and also the lofty goals of the United Nations*" (China. org. cn, 2015). Since then, on many important occasions, President Xi has proposed a series of ideas of a common value for all mankind.

In March 2023, at the Communist Party of China (CPC) in Dialogue with World Political Parties High-level Meeting, when proposing the Global Civilization Initiative (GDI), President Xi stressed that "*peace, development, equity, justice, democracy, and freedom are the common aspirations of all peoples*", and that "*...countries need to keep an open mind in appreciating the*

---

1 The Chinese version of the section was published at *Shaanxi Daily* and is available at http://news.xjtu.edu.cn/info/1033/190808.htm.

perceptions of values by different civilizations, and refrain from imposing their own values or models on others..." (Chinadaily.com, 2023).

The common values of humanity embody the values commonly pursued by people in different countries. Among them, peace and development are the common goals of mankind, equity and justice are the common ideals of mankind, and democracy and freedom are the common pursuits of mankind. The common values shared by all mankind are the foundation of the values recognized across countries, transcending any ideological differences, social system variations, and levels of development (Qstheory.cn, 2022).

The common values of humanity are embedded in Chinese civilization. Advocating benevolence, prioritizing people's well-being, maintaining integrity, respecting justice, valuing harmony and cooperation, and aspiring to great unity are essential Chinese cultural values; they are also values shared by all civilizations in the world. As we have discussed in this course, "benevolence, righteousness, courtesy, wisdom, and trustworthiness" (*ren yi li zhi xin*), "seeking common ground while reserving differences" (*qiu tong cun yi*), and "harmony between human and nature" (*tian ren he yi*) are examples of China's excellent traditional culture. These values are symbols of Chinese civilization and are Chinese wisdom contributing to human civilization.

To promote the common values of humanity, it is important to share with the world China's excellent traditional culture, as well as to develop intercultural education with Chinese characteristics. This will help the world better understand Chinese cultural values, thereby gaining a deeper understanding of contemporary China's social, political, economic, and cultural development.

The common values of humanity do not deny the diversity of civilizations and cultures. Rather, by upholding the principles of equality, mutual learning, dialogue, and inclusiveness, these common values respect the differences in cultural values shared by people in different countries. Adhering to the principle of harmony in diversity, the pursuit of common values requires active exchanges and mutual learning among different countries and cultures. Through these exchanges and mutual learning, the pursuit of common values enhances friendship between peoples, drives human progress, and acts as a bond for maintaining world peace.

Moreover, the promotion of common values of humanity acknowledges the interdependence of countries. Through pursuing peace, development, equity, justice, democracy, and freedom, the promotion of common values stresses the significance of shared global responsibilities to promote global development and achieve sustainable development of all cultural groups together. Hence, it contributes to the building of a community with a shared future for mankind through exchanges and mutual learning among civilizations.

4.6 Chapter Summary

In this chapter, we introduced the definitions of values. The chapter then reviewed Chinese and Western values as summarized by non-empirically based teaching materials. We also reviewed the research findings on Chinese and Western values, as represented by Hofstede's value dimensions. We would like to remind students that, insightful as it is, the Hofstede's work is problematic. Adopting a limited number of fixed, over-simplified and over-generalized descriptions of national values, Hofstede's work involves stereotypes and can easily lead to ethnocentric, Eurocentric and cultualist prejudice. In sharp contrast is the proposal of common values of all mankind. The promotion of common values of all mankind recognizes the richness of world cultures while acknowledging the openness and exchanges of cultures throughout human history.

4.7 Case Study Assignment

Please write an essay, explaining how you think of the following material, and why. Your essay should be no less than 300 words, should be well-argued, well organized and clearly written, and should contain few grammar, syntax, or spelling errors.

> 社会学家简单地将世界分为个人主义和集体主义两个阵营，也就是西方个人主义与东方集体主义阵营……这两种相互对立的社会模式对于社会学分析是大有裨益的，但是在个人和跨文化方面，二分法而不是连续性的分析模式是失之偏颇的。例如，日本社会学家杉本认为将日本归类为绝对的集体主义文化是有违事实的。不可否认，日本社会中，集体主义扮演着重要角色，但是要说这是日本或东方社会的特性，他表示怀疑。他指出，实际上，这因人而异，有的日本人集体主义多一点，有的则个人主义多一点。他认为，对于日本文化，还有另外一个误解，那就是认为集体主义统治日本，而不以时间、地点、历史条件为转移。

(Kumaravadivelu, 2017, p.11)

References

Berger, P. (1988). An East Asian development model. In P. Berger, H. M. Hsiao (Eds.), *In search of an East Asian development model* (pp. 3-11). Transaction Publishers.

Bloom, R., & Solotko, J. (2003). The foundation of Confucianism in Chinese and Japanese accounting. *Accounting, Business & Financial History, 13*(1), 27-40. https://doi.org/10.1080/0958520021016456c

ChinaDaily.com (2023). Xi attends dialogue between CPC, world political parties. http://www.chinadaily.com.cn/a/202303/15/WS6411b4dda31057c47ebb4ab5_6.html

China.org.cn (2015). Xi's speech at the general debate of the 70 session of the UN general assembly. http://www.china.org.cn/chinese/2015-11/06/content_36999256.htm

Dobewall, H., & Strack, M. (2011). Cultural value differences, value stereotypes, and diverging identities in intergroup conflicts. *International Journal of Conflict and Violence, 5*(1), 211-223. 1. 10.4119/UNIBI/IJCV.73

Fang, T. (2003). A critique of Hofstede's fifth national culture dimension. *International Journal of Cross-cultural Management, 3*(3), 347-368. https://doi.org/ 10.1177/1470595803003003006

Fang, T. (2005). From "onion" to "ocean": Paradox and change in national cultures. *International Studies of Management & Organization, 35*(4): 71-90. https://doi.org/10.1080/ 00208825.2005.11043743

Ho, D. Y. F. (1998). Interpersonal relationships and relationship dominance: An analysis based on methodological relationalism. *Asian Journal of Social Psychology, 1*(1): 1-16. https://doi.org/10.1111/1467-839x.00002

Ho, D. Y. F., Fu, W., & Ng S. M. (2004). Guilt, shame and embarrassment: Revelations of face and self. *Culture & Psychology, 10*(1): 64-84. https://doi.org/ 10.1177/1354067x04044166

Hofstede, G. (1980). *Culture's consequences: International differences in work-related values.* Sage.

Hofstede, G. (2011). Dimensionalizing cultures: The Hofstede model in context. *Online Readings in Psychology and Culture, 2*(1): 2307-0919. https://doi.org/10.9707/2307-0919.1014

Hofstede, G., & Bond, M. (1988). The Confucius connection: From cultural roots to economic growth. *Organizational Dynamics, 16*(4): 5-21. https://doi.org/10.1016/0090-2616(88)90009-5

Hofstede, G., & Minkev, M. (2010). *Cultures and organizations: Software of the mind.* McGraw-Hill.

Holliday, A., Hyde, M., & Kullman, J. (2004). *Intercultural communication: An advanced resource book for students.* Routledge.

Holliday, A., (2005). *The struggle to teach English as an international language.* Oxford University Press.

Hwang, K. (1987). Face and favor: The Chinese power game. *The American Journal of Psychology,* 92(4): 944-974. https://doi.org/10.1086/228588

Knafo, A., Roccas, S., & Sagiv, L. (2011). The value of values in cross-cultural research: A special issue in honor of Shalom Schwartz. *The Journal of Cross-cultural Psychology,* 42(2): 178-185. https://doi.org/10.1177/0022022110396863

Leung, T. K. P., & Chan, R. (2003). Face, favor and positioning: A Chinese power game. *The European Journal of Marketing,* 37(11/12): 1575-1598. https://doi.org/10.1108/03090560310495366

O'sullivan, T., Hartley, J., Saunders, D., Martin, M., & John F. (1994). *Key concepts in communication and cultural studies.* Routledge.

Qstheory.cn. (2022). An Unswerving Champion for Humanity's Common Values. http://news.sohu.com/a/616322162_117159

Sagiv, L., Sverdlik, N., & Schwarz, N. (2011). To compete or to cooperate? Values' impact on perception and action in social dilemma games. *European Journal of Social psychology,* 41(1): 64-77. https://doi.org/10.1002/ejsp.729

Samovar, L., Porter, R., & McDaniel, E. (2012). *Cross-cultural communication.* Peking University Press.

Schwartz, S. H. (1999). A theory of cultural values and some implications for work. *Applied Psychology: An international Review,* 48(1): 23-47. https://doi.org/10.1080/026999499377655

Schwartz, S. H. (2006). A theory of cultural value orientations: Explication and applications. *Comparative Sociology,* 5(2-3): 137-182. https://doi.org/10.1163/156913306778667357

Smith, S., & Smith, P. (2000). Implications for distance education in the study approaches of different Chinese national groups. *Journal of Distance Education,* 15(2): 71-84. https://doi.org/10.1080/0158791990200106

Stephenson, J. (2008). The cultural values model: An integrated approach to values in landscapes. *Landscape and Urban Planning,* 84(2): 127-139. https://doi.org/10.1016/j.landurbplan.2007.07.003

Sung, K. (1998). An exploration of actions of filial piety. *Journal of Aging Studies,* 12(4): 369-386. https://doi.org/10.1016/s0890-4065(98)90025-1

Yang, J. (2016). Comparing values and social codes. In R. Y. Yang & M. Tian (Eds.); *Chinese and Western culture: A comparative approach.* Xian Jiaotong University Press.

Kumaravadivelu, B. (2017) *Cultural globalization and langage education [Wenhua quanqiuhua yu yuyan jiaoyu]* (B. Shao, Trans.). Peking Language and Culture University Press (Original Work Published 2007)

5

Languages and Thinking Patterns

Yang Ruiying

Everyone knows that people from different countries or places may speak differently. Due to the vast difference between English and Chinese, Americans and Chinese cannot communicate in their mother tongue.

People speaking different languages may be different in many aspects as language is one of the most important representations of culture, which means the history, tradition, beliefs and values as well as social codes of a people are usually embedded in the language they speak. Among these differences, the underlying one may be the way they think—the thinking patterns. Thinking patterns can be described as habitual mental processes. At the general level, they can be positive or negative; at a specific level, they can be linear or dialectical, holistic or analytical.

We will start with a brief comparison of the Chinese and English languages—the general and unique structures at the levels of phonology (pronunciation), morphology (word structure) and syntax (sentence structure). We will then move on to a comparison of the differences in the thinking patterns of the peoples.

Activity 5-1 Look at the Chinese expressions and the English translations below, and discuss with your classmates whether there are problems in the translation and what could be the reasons for the problems.

Chinese	English translation
让我们做鸟类的朋友	Let us do the birds friend.
小心滑倒	Slip and fall down carefully.
请带好随身物品	Please take good personal luggage.
先下后上，文明乘车	After first under on, do riding with civility.

5.1 A Brief Definition of Language

If you go out of China to another country, a foreign culture such as Egypt, you would immediately notice the differences in language, architecture style, food and clothes, etc. You would suddenly realize that you could not communicate with the local people with your mother tongue. Since language is the major tool of communication in our life, many people would consider language as a means of communication. However, traffic lights are also a means of communication. In the traffic system of our country, red light means "stop", green light means "go", and yellow light means "prepare to stop". Do you think language is the same as traffic lights? Does the word "red" only have one meaning in a language as in the traffic system? Look at the following examples extracted from an English dictionary:

> With a bright *red* face I was forced to admit that I had no real idea.
>
> He is still vain enough to dye his hair *red*.
>
> The spicy flavors in these dishes call for *reds* rather than whites.
>
> If you go into *the red* you get charged 30p for each transaction.

From these examples, you can see that "red" in English has more than one meaning, so does many other words. Besides, a word in any language can be combined with other words to express complex meaning as in the above examples while it is impossible to have the red and green light on at the same time in the traffic system. So languages and the traffic system are different although they are both developed for communication.

Languages came from the vocal symbols that human ancestors developed for communication thousands of years ago. These symbols are basically arbitrary in relation to the *things* that they refer to, so people living in different cultures have different symbols for the same thing such as *rose* and 玫瑰花. It is possible that they quickly learned to combine the symbols to express more complex meaning. The rules and principles to combine the symbols make the language a system. Therefore, a widely accepted definition of language is: language is a system of arbitrary vocal symbols used for human communication. English and Chinese differ in the linguistic symbols and in the rules and principles to combine the symbols, so the literal translations in Activity 5-1 are inappropriate.

Language is one of the most important human inventions. It represents the identity of a nation and a people, and it is the tool for thinking and communication. For a person as a social being, it is like air. Without it or deprived of it, a person can stop functioning as a social being.

Activity 5-2   Compare the following expressions of "Happy New Year" in different languages and classify them into two groups according to its written form.

新年快乐!

Happy New Year!

新年おめでとうございます！

Bonne Année!

Fröhliches Neujahr!

С новым годом!

Feliz Año Nuevo!

Activity 5-3   Discuss the following questions:

(1) Do you think some languages are more similar than others? Are the languages that look similar spoken by people who live closer geographically?

(2) In what ways English and Chinese differ according to your experience as a native speaker of Chinese and a learner of English?

(3) What roles does language play in your life?

5.2 Language and Language Families

There are many languages in the world. The number is indefinite due to different criteria in classification. Intelligibility, i.e. whether the people involved can understand each other, is one criterion that many linguists use to distinguish language. Although it is difficult to tell the number of languages (approximately 3,000, some put it 5,000), it is possible to classify languages into families, i.e. language families, which is a group of languages related because they are descended from a common ancestor. For example, English belongs to the Indo-European Language family and Chinese to the Sino-Tibetan language family (see Figure 5.1 and Figure 5.2). The Indo-European language family is made up of most of the languages of Europe, the Near East, and India. For example, English belongs to the sub-family of Germanic languages while French belongs to Italic sub-family. That is German and English belong to the same sub-family. The Sino-Tibetan language family consists of Chinese and the Tibeto-Burman languages, which include some 250 languages of East Asia, Southeast Asia and parts of South Asia. They are second only to the Indo-European languages in terms of the number of native speakers.

When the ancestors of a language family moved away from the original homeland territories, they took with them the parent language. Then due to communication difficulty (caused by natural barrier like big mountain or river in the past) between groups of people and isolated development along different lines over a very long period of time, there arose different dialects or varieties. These varieties can gradually become different languages, the process of which can be accelerated by political factors. Although, the members of one language family can be considered as different languages, they tend to share more similarities than those between two languages across family. For instance, there are more differences between Chinese and English than those between English and German.

There are many varieties of English—American English, British English, Singapore English, Indian English, etc. What are the differences between these different varieties of English? Suppose speakers of these different varieties of English were isolated and did not have any means to communicate with each other, do you think that the difference between each of the variety will become bigger and bigger? And do you believe that the speakers of one variety will not be able to understand that of another 2, 000 years later?

Similarly, if speakers of two languages are in close contact, there will be influence in both ways. Some of you who know both English and French may have the feeling that these two languages share many words such as "revolution" "table", etc. One of the reasons is that England was under the rule of a French King after the Norman Conquest in 1066 for over 100 years and many French words entered into the vocabulary of English at that time, and also a lot of new ideas during the Renaissance period went into England through France. If we look at the changes in Chinese language in the last one hundred years, we would also find there are influences from English and other Western languages, especially at the word level, due to the more and more frequent contact between China and the West.

Figure 5.1

The Indo-European language family

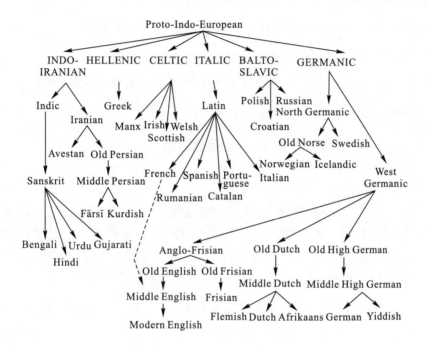

(Adapted from Indo-European languages in *Encyclopedia Britannica*.)

Figure 5.2

Major branches of Tibeto-Burman

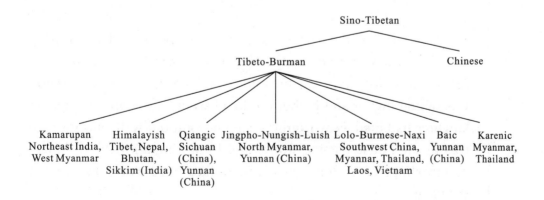

(Tibeto-Burman languages from *Encyclopedia Britannica*)

5.3 Differences between English and Chinese

Activity 5-4   Please read and compare the following Chinese text and its English translation. Then answer the following questions:

(1) How do the two texts differ in the form of nouns?

(2) How do they differ in verb forms?

(3) Is there the same number of subjects in the two texts?

(4) Is the number of sentences in the two texts similar?

(5) What problems do you have in counting the number of sentences?

(6) What are the typical sentence pattern in English and Chinese?

荷塘月色

朱自清

这几天心里颇不宁静。今晚在院子里坐着乘凉，忽然想起日日走过的荷塘，在这满月的光里，总该另有一番样子吧。月亮渐渐地升高了，墙外马路上孩子们的欢笑，已经听不见了；妻在屋里拍着闰儿，迷迷糊糊地哼着眠歌。我悄悄地披了大衫，带上门出去。

沿着荷塘，是一条曲折的小煤屑路。这是一条幽僻的路；白天也少人走，夜晚更加寂寞。荷塘四周，长着许多树，蓊蓊(wěng)郁郁的。路的一旁，是些杨柳，和一些不知道名字的树。没有月光的晚上，这路上阴森森的，有些怕人。今晚却很好，虽然月光也还是淡淡的。

The Lotus Pool by Moonlight

(Translator unknown)

The last few days have found me very restless. This evening as I sat in the yard to enjoy the cool, it struck me how different the lotus pool I pass every day must look under a full moon. The moon was sailing higher and higher up the heavens, the sound of childish laughter had died away from the lane beyond our wall, and my wife was in the house patting Runer and humming a lullaby to him. I quietly slipped on a long gown, and walked out leaving the door on the latch.

A cinder-path winds along by the side of the pool. It is off the beaten track and few pass this way even by day, so at night it is still quieter. Trees grow thick and bosky all around the pool, with willows and other trees I cannot name by the path. On nights when there is no moon the track is almost terrifyingly dark, but tonight it was quite clear, though the moonlight was pale.

5.3.1 Tone vs. stress and one syllable word vs. multi-syllable word

If you read aloud the original Chinese prose and the English translation, what you can notice at the pronunciation level is that Chinese character has tone, while English word has stress in addition to the differences of speech sounds. Also most English words contain more than one syllable while Chinese characters are mono-syllabic. Due to the big difference in pronunciation between English and Chinese, many of you learning English as a foreign language have difficulty in mastering word stress in English and many English speakers learning Chinese find it very difficult to acquire the tones of Chinese characters.

5.3.2 Inflectional vs. non-inflectional at the morphological (word) level

Inflection means the change of word form to indicate grammatical meaning. One of the difference in the forms of nouns and verbs between English and Chinese is caused by the fact that English is an inflectional language while Chinese is a non-inflectional language. The former has the grammatical relations expressed by inflectional endings while the latter does not have changes in word form for the purpose of expressing grammatical meaning.

Table 5.1 Differences in word forms between the two texts

Noun		Verb	
Chinese	English	Chinese	English
天	days	坐着	sat
荷塘	the pool	升高了	was sailing higher and higher up the heavens
月亮	the moon	已经听不见了	had died away
欢笑	laughter	拍着	patting
眠歌	a lullaby	哼着	humming
小煤屑路	a cinder-path	长着	grow
幽僻的路	off the beaten track	是	was
许多树	trees		
杨柳	willows		

Table 5.1 shows that nouns and verbs in English need to be changed in form to indicate plural number and past time while nouns and verbs in Chinese do not undergo any change of form to express the same meanings. For example, in English it is necessary to vary between "one day" and "two days", "sit" and "sat", while in Chinese the word "天" remains the same no matter whether it is singular or plural, so does the verb "坐". This kind of difference in the forms of nouns and verbs between English and Chinese is caused by the property of inflection.

Although the inflectional endings of English are very complicated in comparison to Chinese, English has only kept inflections to the third person singular (I sing, you sing, he sings) and to verbs of past tense and perfect aspect. If we compare English with French, German or Spanish, English is much simpler because it has dropped many grammatical inflections. French and German have kept many more inflections than English. The following is the change of verbs in Italian in correspondence to the number and person of pronoun:

lo parlo (I speak)	noi parliamo (we speak)
tu parli (you speak)	voi parlate (you speak)
lui/lei parla (he/she speaks)	loro parlono (they speak)

5.3.3 Compounding vs. derivation in word construction

As shown in Table 5.2, Chinese words may be constructed by adding a modifier to a general word such as "公牛", "母牛", "小牛" while the corresponding words in English are single words like "bull", "cow", and "calf". You can also find similar words like "白酒", "红酒", "啤酒", "卡车", "出租车", "公交车", "小轿车", etc. All these Chinese words are constructed by combining a modifying word indicating its particular feature and a general word indicating its family. But the corresponding English words do not share this kind of construction method. In the case of animal names such as "ox", English borrowed "beef" and "cattle" from French, while "ox", "calf" and "cow" are from old English. Due to its close contact with Roman Empire and France in its history, English borrowed a large number of words from Latin and French. In addition to borrowing, the bulk of English words are formed by derivation such as "beauty", "beautiful", "beautifully"; "like", "likely" and "dislike". However, for Chinese, the bulk of words are constructed by putting two or more words together, i.e. compounding. Although English can also build words by compounding such as "raincoat" and "notebook", etc. , it is not the primary method.

The difference in the primary method of word construction leads to a large number of independent words in English. This partly explains why English has a very large vocabulary and vocabulary learning is very difficult for foreign learners. If you want to be able to read English newspaper without difficulty, you would need to have an English vocabulary of about 6,000 words. While in the case of Chinese, having a command of about 2,000 characters would be able to understand most of the articles in Chinese newspapers because the majority of words are constructed from a limited number of characters. But learning to construct words from characters is a very demanding task for foreign learners. In China's primary schools, teaching students to construct idiomatic words and phrases is one of the central aims of the course of Chinese language.

Table 5.2 Comparison of a word formation method in Chinese and English

牛	公牛	母牛	小牛	牛肉	野牛
cattle, ox	bull, ox	cow	calf	beef	buffalo
猪	公猪	母猪	小猪	猪肉	野猪
pig, swine	boar	sow	piglet	pork	wild boar
羊	公羊	母羊	小羊	羊肉	山羊
sheep	ram	ewe	lamb	mutton	goat

5.3.4 Subject-prominent vs. topic-prominent in terms of syntactic structure

The primary order of English sentence is subject + verb + object, i.e. SVO language. This is also the case with many sentences in Chinese. However, there are also many sentences in Chinese without a subject.

For example:

> 东西放在柜子里了。
> Everything has been put in the cupboard.
>
> (Yip & Rimmington, 1997, p.109)
>
> 懒惰是不对的。
> Being lazy is wrong.
>
> (ibid)
>
> 这棵树叶子很大。
> The leaves of this tree are very big.
>
> (Li & Thompson, 1981, p.15)

> 张三我已经见过了。
> I have already seen Zhangsan.

(ibid)

You probably think the noun phrases located at the beginning of the above sentences are subjects. The widely accepted definition of subject is *"the noun or pronoun representing the initiator or recipient of the action (or non-action) expressed by the verb."* (Yip & Rimmington, 1997, p.109). The noun phrases at the beginning of the above sentences are not the doers of actions, so they are not the subjects. Linguists of Chinese language (e.g. Yip & Rimmington, 1997; Li & Thompson, 1981) would consider the noun phrase in each of the above sentence as the topic, and the rest are comment. That is in the language of Chinese there are two primary sentence patterns: subject + predicate (verb/verb phrase) and topic + comment.

It is observed that the topic-comment structure is generally used when the speaker and listener share the contextual knowledge and the subject, topic and object are known to them. So a second important factor in determining the basic order of sentence in Chinese is meaning in addition to grammatical relation with respect to the verb. This is a unique syntactic feature of Putonghua (Li & Thompson, 1981).

5.3.5 Hypotactic (form-focused) vs. paratactic (meaning-focused)

This phenomenon is related to the fact that English focuses on form, involving agreement between different elements in a sentence and the completeness of syntactic structure. Violation of these rules leads to ungrammatical sentences. For example, a grammatical English sentence must have a subject and a predicate. But Chinese tends to focus on the communication of meaning, so if the meaning is clear in the context, the omission of subject or predicate would be acceptable. There is no strict requirement on form, i.e. the issue of agreement and the fixed subject and predicate syntactic structure. Now look at the Chinese poem by Jia Dao in the Tang Dynasty and its English translation:

> 松下问童子，　　Beneath the pines **I** look for the recluse,
> 言师采药去。　　His page replies: "Gathering herbs my master's away.
>
> 只在此山中，　　**You** will find him nowhere, as close are the clouds,
> 云深不知处。　　Though **he** must be on the hill, **I** dare say."

You can see that in the English translation of this poem, the translator added subjects for every sentence while in the original Chinese poem, there is no explicit subject because it is understood that in the context readers would understand that the author is the subject. The omission of subject is very common in Chinese texts while it is very rare in English. Even in English poems, the omission of subject is also very rare. The following is the first verse of a poem by the famous English poet Robert Burns (1759–1796):

> **A Red, Red Rose**
>
> O, my luve's like a red, red rose,
> That's newly sprung in June;
> O, my luve's like the melodie,
> That's sweetly played in tune.
> As fair art thou, my bonnie lass,
> So deep in luve am I;
> And I will luve thee still, my dear,
> Till a' the seas gang dry.

The differences in terms of subjects as shown above are due to the different rules of sentence construction in English and Chinese. English sentence must have a subject and a predicate, and it must have only one subject and one predicate, which is joined according to the rule of agreement. For Chinese sentences, the subject is optional. When the subject and topic are understood in the context, the speaker can omit the subject and can also use the topic-comment sentence pattern.

5.3.6 Hierarchical vs. linear structure

English sentence generally consists of a subject and a predicate (verb or verbal phrase). The predicate is the focus of the sentence, which the other elements hang to. If it is necessary to modify the subject, predicate or object, sub-clauses are used and a complex sentence is constructed. However, in the same context, a series of parallel clauses may be used in Chinese along with the development of the event. In the following example from Lu Xun's work, you can see that one sentence in Chinese is translated into four English sentences with four explicit subjects.

For example:

> 当她初到的时候，四叔虽然照例皱过眉，但鉴于向来雇用女工之难，也就并不大反对，只是暗暗地告诫四婶说，这种人似乎很可怜，但是伤风败俗的，用她帮忙还可以，祭祀时候可用不着她沾手，一切饭菜，只好自己做，否则，不干不净，祖宗是不吃的。

> Though my uncle has frowned as before when she first arrived, **they** always have such trouble finding servants that he raised no serious objections, simply warning his wife on the quiet that while such people might be very pathetic they exerted a bad moral influence. **She** could work for them but must have nothing to do with ancestral sacrifices. **They** would have to prepare all the dishes themselves. Otherwise **they** would be unclean and the ancestors would not accept them.

(Translated by Yang Xianyi & Gladys Yang)

5.3.7 Low-context vs. high-context

Although language is universally considered as the tool of communication, the crucial element of communication—meaning making does not only rely on linguistic forms. It also relies on the context of communication, which includes the culture, situation, and relationship between the two parties in communication. That is the shared information.

For example:

> Fall Baby Sale
>
> Which of your people is the fish?

It is not possible to decide what the above two sentences mean because you are not given the cultural and context knowledge. In fact, context plays a role in communication in all languages. But some languages are less dependent on the context, some are more dependent. If we compare French, English and Chinese on a continuum between low-context and high-context, English should be in the middle, French at the end of low context while Chinese at the end of high context.

For example:

> 她女儿比我大。
>
> (a) Her daughter is older than mine.
>
> (b) Her daughter is older than me.

Which English translation given above is correct? If the hearer knows that the speaker has a daughter, he/she may come up with (a), or vice versa. The English sentences avoided the ambiguity by distinguishing the cases of possessive and genitive, but Chinese does not have the category of case. The understanding of the above sentence in Chinese mainly depends on the context—the shared knowledge between the speaker and listener. This is the characteristic of a high-context language. In fact, the possible omission of sentence subject in Chinese is also a feature of high-context language.

5.3.8 Alphabetical vs. orthographic

English is an alphabetical language, and the writing system of which consists of 26 letters. The letters are highly arbitrary, and the words bear no relationship with the objects or things they represent. However, some characters created in the early time of Chinese bear close resemblance to the objects they represented. These Chinese characters are descriptive, which are considered hieroglyphic characters. Figure 5.3 shows the development process of a few typical hieroglyphic characters in Chinese. In addition to these hieroglyphic characters, there are many other characters created with different methods such as combination of two independent morphemes, one representing the image (meaning), the other representing the pronunciation. Nowadays, the majority of Chinese characters are no longer direct descriptions of the objects they represent. But in general, Chinese characters are representations of meaning in one way or the other.

Figure 5.3
Illustration of the difference in writing system

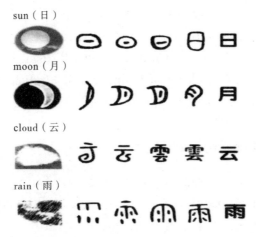

So far, we have briefly discussed the main differences between English and Chinese in structure at various levels. It is likely that these differences are related with the perspectives that a people get to know the outside world. Once the language is developed and stabilized, it can influence the way that we perceive the world. Along this line of thinking, Chinese people, with a language focusing more on meaning than form, tends to think holistically, while English people, with a language focusing on form with inflectional endings and agreement requirement, tend to think analytically. We will discuss thinking and thinking patterns in the next section.

5.4 Thinking and Thinking Patterns

As given at the beginning of this chapter, thinking patterns can be considered as habitual mental processes. However, the mental activity cannot be seen. Our mind is like a black box. How can we reveal the habitual mental processes? Let us look at a few positions on the roles of languages in relation to the study of other issues:

John Locke (1632–1704), British philosopher, argued that "*the use of words ... stands, as outward Marks of our internal Ideas*" (Baghramian,1998, XXX).

John Austin, a professor of philosophy at Oxford University in 1950s, held the view that "*the common stock of knowledge that has been handed down from generation to generation through established linguistic usage, is a reliable but under-used source of philosophical illumination*" (Austin in Baghramian,1998, pp.108–109).

The above quotations from famous philosophers point to the meaning that accumulated knowledge by generations was recorded by language, and language can be used as a primary source to study the mental activity of its users or other issues. So in what follows, we will discuss the internal mental activity—the modes of thinking of Chinese and English speakers in relation to the typical characteristics of English and Chinese languages.

5.4.1 Analytical vs. holistic

As discussed above, English focuses more on form, involving agreement between different elements in a sentence and the completeness of the syntactic structure, while Chinese focuses more on meaning and on the context of communication, without inflectional endings and strict requirement of subject and predicate in sentences. As people live in their linguistic environment all the time, they tend to perceive the world and think in the way predisposed in the language. Along this line of argument, English speakers tend to discern and categorize the object, and then to break it down into smaller constituents/units to study. They like to find out how the particular object is structured and whether it can be further broken down. However, Chinese speakers would tend to observe an "object" as a whole, and in relationship to the other items in the system. (Nisbett, 2003).

The practice of Western and Chinese medicine is an example that can illustrate the working of analytical and holistic thinking modes. The Western medicine classifies human diseases into many different categories and study each as thorough as possible. Doctors of Chinese medicine tend to study disease in relation to the environment and the life style, and they are inclined to see a human body as a system of its own and as a part of the surrounding environment.

5.4.2 Deductive vs. inductive thinking

> ... The most striking difference between the traditions at the two ends of the civilized world is in the destiny of logic. For the West, logic has been central and the thread of transmission has never snapped ...
>
> —Philosopher Angus Graham

Deductive thinking begins with a claim or proposition which is believed to be true or self-evident, and then moves to a more specific conclusion. It is based on logic rather than evidence. The process of deduction is usually illustrated with a syllogism, a three-part set of statements or propositions that include a major premise, a minor premise, and a conclusion.

For example:

> Major Premise: All books from that store are new.
>
> Minor Premise: These books are from that store.
>
> Conclusion: Therefore, these books are new.
>
> All oranges are fruits.
>
> All fruits grow on trees.
>
> Therefore, all oranges grow on trees.
>
> (Source: http://www.buzzle.com)

Deductive reasoning is more direct and to the point although it can sometimes be invalid if the conclusion does not follow the premise. A sound syllogism must be both true and valid. In the example below, the major premise is not true, and it leads to an invalid conclusion.

For example:

> Major premise: All politicians are male.
>
> Minor premise: Barbara Boxer is a politician.
>
> Conclusion: Therefore, Barbara Boxer is male.

However, inductive reasoning moves from specific facts, observations, or experience to a general conclusion. According to formal logic, the conclusion of inductive reasoning can only be an inference, which is not conclusive because it is not possible to establish cause-effect relation (Kirszner & Mandell, 2008).

For example:

> All the swans that I have seen are white in color.
>
> Therefore, all swans are white.

The problem with the above reasoning is that the swans that being seen may be a small and unrepresentative set, so the conclusion is overgeneralized, i.e. a hasty generalization.

5.4.3 Linear vs. dialectical

Westerners tend to believe that the world is composed of discrete objects and they understand the rules that govern them and their attributes. Therefore, they are likely to think in a linear mode. They like *either/or* instead of *both/and*.

"*But the eastern tradition of thought emphasizes the constantly changing nature of reality. The world is not static but dynamic and changeable. Being in a given state is just a sign that the state is about to change*" (Nisbett, 2003, p.174). Because of this inclination, it is easier for them to perceive the signs of changing and to tolerate ambiguities and to favor "middle way". These differences can be perceived in the idioms in the two languages.

For example:

English	Chinese
Half a loaf is better than none.	Too humble is half-proud.
One against all is certain to fall.	Beware of your friends, not your enemies.
"For example" is no proof.	A man is stronger than iron and weaker than a fly.

(Nisbett, 2003, p.173)

5.4.4 Abstract vs. imagery

It is generally believed that speakers of alphabetical languages are likely to neglect form or shape of the symbol because there are no relationship between the linguistic signs and the objects, while speakers of non-alphabetical languages tend to pay more attention to the image because the linguistic symbols represent the shape or meaning of the objects to some extent. For instance, the word "table" bears no relationship to the object, but the Chinese character "桌子" is a combination of the shape and material that a table is made of. Although the majority of Chinese characters are not pictographs anymore, they are ideograms, with a complex form. This characteristic can implicitly direct its speakers' attention to images. So speakers of English have the advantage in generalization and abstraction, and speakers of Chinese pay more attention to the image or shape of things, thus more likely to think visually. The art of Chinese calligraphy might be related to this thinking pattern.

5.5 The Relationship Between Language and Thought

In 1929, Edward Sapir, a famous anthropologist wrote:

> Human beings do not live in the objective world alone, nor in the world of social activity as ordinarily understood, but are very much at the mercy of the particular language which has become the medium of expression for their society ... We see and hear and otherwise experience very largely as we do because the language habits of our community predispose certain choices of interpretation
>
> (Sapir, 1929, as cited in Wardhaugh, 1992, p.218).

Benjamin Whorf made even stronger claims:

> The background linguistic system (in other words, the grammar) of each language is not merely the reproducing instrument for voicing ideas but rather is itself the shaper of ideas, the program and guide for the individual's mental activity, for his analysis of impressions, for his synthesis of his mental stock in trade ... We dissect nature along lines laid down by our native languages
>
> (Carrol, 1956, p.212, as cited in Wardhaugh, 1991, p.219).

Whorf's viewpoint is that the language we speak determines how we perceive and think about the world. That is people speaking different languages must perceive and think about world in different ways. For example, Chinese language does not have the grammatical category subjunctive mood in Chinese, so Chinese people would not be able to think hypothetically. Chinese language does not have inflectional verb marking to indicate tense, can we conclude that Chinese people cannot perceive time? The answer is certainly negative. "*If speakers were not able to think about something for which their language had not a specific word, translations would be impossible, as would learning a second language*" (Fromkin, 2007, p.27).

Although, linguistic determinism has been challenged continuously, there is still evidence that speakers of different languages tend to think about the world in different ways as a result of differences in languages. For example, the inflectional property of English may have promoted analytical thinking to a certain extent, while the linear syntactic structure of Chinese, with a focus on event structure in experience might have strengthened inductive thinking, and also its stronger dependence on context may have fostered dialectical and holistic thinking. We can, in general, postulate that language probably plays a role in helping to focus attention and to stabilize the different orientations throughout life, but it does not play a deterministic role in the ways of thinking.

Although this chapter has focused on the differences between languages and modes of thinking, it is necessary to emphasize that these differences do not form closed compartments, and people can develop awareness of the differences and go beyond them.

5.6 Chapter Summary

This chapter has compared the main systematic differences between

English and Chinese languages in pronunciation, word formation, sentence structure and their dependence on context in communication. It is expected that these comparisons can provide a glimpse of the linguistic resources that different languages make use of. For example, compounding and derivation are both resources for word formation, but Chinese language prefers to use the former while English prefers to use the latter. However, this does not mean that Chinese language does not have derivative words and English does not have compound words. They both make use of the same linguistic resources in different ways.

The differences in the modes of thinking are also general inclinations developed in the long tradition of a culture. In the current inter-connected world, there are many opportunities for people to learn from other culture through education or work, so those inclinations can not always be applied to individuals. However, being aware of the existence of different modes of thinking can be useful in understanding possible problems in cross-cultural communication, and in the development of open-mindness and creativity.

5.7 Case Study Assignments

Assignment 5-1 Read the poem and answer the questions below.

《天净沙·秋思》	Autumn Thoughts
马致远	*(Translated by Xu Yuanchong)*
枯藤老树昏鸦，	Over old trees wreathed with rotten vines fly evening crows;
小桥流水人家，	Under a small bridge near a cottage stream flows;
古道西风瘦马。	On ancient road in the west wind a lean horse goes.
夕阳西下，断肠人在天涯。	Westward declines the sun; Far, far from home is the heartbroken one.

Questions:

(1) Are there any verbs in the original Chinese poem?

(2) Are there any verbs in the English translation? What are they?

(3) What elements were added in the English translation?

(4) How do you evaluate the English translation of the famous Chinese poem?

(5) How can you account for the differences between the original Chinese poem and the English translation?

Assignment 5-2   Identify the differences in the organization of the email messages below and discuss what is the underlying thinking pattern of each text.

Text A

Dear Professor Allison,

   I have been interested in your work on cross-cultural communication for some time. I am currently studying for my MA in the program of English Literature at Xi'an Jiaotong University, and will graduate next year. After graduation, I plan to pursue PhD degree in the field of cross-cultural communication under your supervision. However, I am not sure whether you have the quota to take in graduate students from overseas next year. Would you please let me know whether I have an opportunity if I apply? I am looking forward to hearing from you soon. Thank you very much!

Yours sincerely,

Hui Jia

Text B

Dear Professor Allison,

   I am writing to inquire whether you have the quota to take in overseas graduate students next year. I am currently studying for my MA in the program of English Literature at Xi'an Jiaotong University and will graduate next year. I have been interested in your work on cross-cultural communication for some time. So after graduation, I plan to pursue PhD degree in the field of cross-cultural communication under your supervision. Would you please let me know whether I have an opportunity if I apply? I am looking forward to hearing from you soon. Thank you very much!

Yours sincerely,

Hui Jia

References

Baghramian, M. (1998). *Modern philosophy of language.* J. M. Dent.

Fromkin, V., Rodman, R., & Hyams, N. (2007). *An introduction to language.* Peking University Press.

Kirszner, L., & Mandell, S. (2008). *The Wadsworth handbook.* China Renmin University Press.

Indo-European languages. (2021). In Encyclopædia Britannica. http://academic.eb.cnpeak.com/levels/collegiate/article/Indo-European-languages/109767

Li, C. N., & Thompson, S. A. (1981). *Mandarin Chinese.* University of California Press.

Nisbett, R. (2003). *The geography of thought.* The Free Press.

Wardhaugh, R. (1992). *An introduction to sociolinguistics (2nd edition).* Blackwell.

Tibeto-Yip, P., & Rimmington, D. (1997). *Chinese: An essential grammar.* Routledge.

Tibeto-Burman languages: Relationships among the Tibeto-Burman languages. In Encyclopædia Britannica. http://academic.eb.cnpeak.com/levels/collegiate/assembly/view/119281

6

Perspectives on Education: A Comparative Approach

Carla Briffett–Aktaş

What do you think of when you hear or read "education"? We often associate this word with other terms, like school, teacher, or student. Many of our experiences in life have taken place in formal education. That is why we connect the above words. Formal education takes place in institutions such as primary or secondary schools. These institutions are compulsory in most countries, meaning that by law, children must attend these different levels of schooling. Universities and vocational education also occur in formal educational institutions but are not compulsory. Although these higher levels of education are not legally required, most people view post-compulsory formal education as crucial for obtaining employment and securing a stable financial future. Formal education involves students learning from teachers (compulsory schooling) or instructors, lecturers, or professors (post-compulsory education).[1] What about before we enter formal education or in our social lives? Does this mean we only receive education in school buildings from designated educators? No, we learn from the moment we are born. We learn languages and how to walk, read, and write letters or characters before we enter formal education. Likewise, when we are students in different levels of formal education, we do not stop learning once we exit the school building. Those around us teach us all the time. For example, a friend showing you how to use a new APP or learning how to play a musical instrument from a website

---

1 In post-compulsory education, educators are comprised of instructors, lecturers, or professors depending on their level of education and position within the university. It is for this reason that all three terms are used interchangeably throughout this chapter.

are examples of informal education. In informal education, we are students who obtain new knowledge and skills, but our "teachers" are not educators doing their job. In this case, your teacher can be your parent, friend, or someone you meet who teaches you something. Education does not only happen in a classroom. It can and does happen at all times, everywhere. This is what Confucius meant when he wrote,

> The Master said, 'When I walk along with two others, they may serve me as my teachers. I will select their good qualities and follow them, their bad qualities and avoid them' (子曰："三人行，必有我师焉。择其善者而从之，其不善者而改之。")
>
> (*The Analects*, VII-22).

We are all life-long learners and have many educators throughout our lives. Even into adulthood, learning does not stop. Our teachers also change depending on the situation. For example, a student teaching a lecturer or professor in a university class how to operate a piece of new technology becomes a teacher, and the lecturer or professor becomes a student. We are always students, learning new things and ideas.

Formal education plays a significant role in our lives because our attendance in educational institutions is where we spend most of our waking time during childhood, adolescence, and young adulthood, shaping who we become later in life. Educational researchers and educators often participate in comparative education studies to improve and develop formal education for students. Manzon (2011) describes comparative education as a

> subfield of education studies that systematically examines educational systems and their relations with intra- and extra-educational phenomena within and among two or more nations. Its specific object is "educational systems" and the interactions among them, examined from a cross-cultural (or cross-national, cross-regional, cross-societal) perspective through the systematic use of the comparative method (emphasis in the original)
>
> (p. 171).

Comparing education systems allows educational practitioners and policymakers to share classroom practices with other colleagues, exchange ideas that can improve curricula (documents that outline what students are required to learn), make sure that student achievement is on par with international student performance, and identify areas in education systems that need improvement. Comparative education can use different comparison methods, such as geographical location, time, gender, culture, policies, and values (Bray et al., 2014). The primary goal of comparative education is to improve education at all levels.

When comparing education systems, the first step is to develop reflective practices. This means that we should reflect on our education system, educational experiences, methods of instruction, curricula, and policy. Reflective practices will allow us to identify what we are doing well and where improvement may be needed. Kolb (1984) borrowed Lewin's feedback model from engineering to outline how we develop and implement reflective practice. First, we have "*concrete experiences,*" we observe and reflect on those experiences, we form "*abstract concepts and generalizations,*" and finally, we test the "*implications of concepts in new situations*" (Kolb, 1984, p. 21). Through reflective practices, we can learn from others. The same process can be applied to a variety of areas of education.

Figure 6.1
Reflective practice example 1

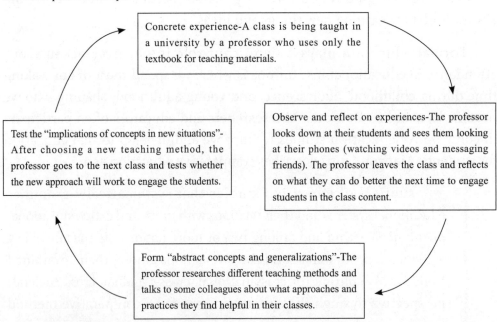

(Kolb, 1984, p. 21).

The first reflective example improved the professor's teaching style and methodology. The second example taught the student the importance of time management and organization, skills necessary throughout that student's academic and future work life. When we compare education systems, the reflective practice is on a bigger scale but follows the same general patterns. Throughout the following comparisons between Chinese and Western education systems and ideas, reflect on your educational experience.

Figure 6.2
Reflective practice example 2

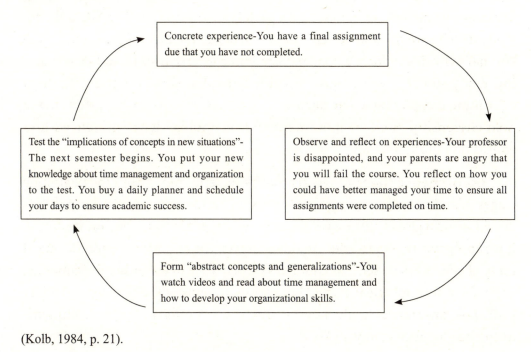

(Kolb, 1984, p. 21).

6.1 Abstract Conceptualization

This section will introduce you to several valuable concepts that will help you analyze the literature presented in Section 6.3. The theoretical concepts are essentialism, globalization, and convergence theory.

Essentialism is *"the idea that things have basic characteristics that make them what they are"* and *"that groups of people…have different characteristics that cannot be changed"* (*Cambridge Dictionary*, 2023). Essentialism ignores the complexity and nuance of people, groups, and societies. For example, when traveling to a new country, if we assume that the citizens of that country will be completely different from us, this is an essentialist mistake. There are always common aspects or characteristics between people, regardless of their cultural or social background.

Globalization refers to the interconnectedness and interdependence of people and countries worldwide in *"political, technological and cultural, as well as economic"* domains (Giddens, 2002, p. 10). Education has experienced globalization trends, with academic exchanges becoming options of study for university students and knowledge becoming easily accessible through technology development. For example, the University Alliance of the Silk

Road (UASR), based at Xi'an Jiaotong University, includes more than 100 universities and offers collaboration and exchange opportunities as well as summer online lecture courses in a variety of disciplines (UASR, n.d.) for students who are not able to relocate for an academic exchange physically but still have the desire for a globalized academic experience. In addition, many university students will choose to study abroad at some point during their education, completing whole degree programs in countries where they do not hold citizenship. Student movement and technology have influenced how education is done globally.

Convergence theory suggests that as societies move from the beginning stages of industrialization to become highly industrialized, similar patterns develop, and a global culture will form (Kneissel et al., 1974; Outhwaite, 2016). If we apply this theory to educational contexts, the argument would be one of unity of education systems as countries engage with one another in economic, social, and technological terms. Education systems will begin to look more similar as governments, education systems, and professors prepare students to enter a global economy and society.

Using a dialectic approach can be a helpful tool for analyzing such complex topics. Dialectics was used by Socrates and Plato in ancient Greece. *"It is essentially posing of a question,…its interrogation and clarification with a view to arriving at a positive conclusion"* (Jenkins, 2018, p. i). This method will help us challenge the stereotypes and biases of Western and Chinese educational systems by asking:

> — Is the information presented accurate or based on stereotypes and biases?
>
> — What key points can we learn from each other to better education?

6.2 Concrete experience

Activity 6-1 Think about your life so far. Can you think of examples of your formal and informal education? Who are some of your informal teachers? What did they teach you? Has formal or informal education had a more significant impact on your life? How so?

Activity 6-2 What are some advantages of comparing students, educators, and education systems in different regions? Do you think there are differences between Chinese and Western education in terms of the purposes of education, teaching and learning styles, and assessment practices? If yes, what are the differences?

Activity 6-3   In 2022, CGTN conducted a panel discussion titled "How does China's education system work?" outlining the changing Chinese education landscape and comparing it with Western educational practices. Please watch the panel discussion. What are the differences outlined? How would you evaluate the video? Do you agree or disagree with the differences highlighted?

6.3 Reflective observation and comparison

Educational practices in different regions of the world are compared using different criteria. Comparing higher education systems and classroom practices aims to improve formal education by learning what other education systems and educators do for their students that work well and adopting these practices in our education systems, universities, and classrooms. We can also understand different people's perspectives and ways of knowing and being in the world. We must be cautious that the dominant views are accurate and that comparisons do not lead to stereotyping. Education and educational practices vary from one city, province, or country to another. Generalizations are okay to understand the education systems being examined broadly, but we must critically evaluate the literature and explore the complex reasons behind scholarly perceptions and observations. The comparisons made in this section between Western and Chinese education illustrate the dichotomies often used to compare educational systems rather than to make definitive judgments about any particular system.

The chapter begins by outlining dominant views of Western and Chinese education regarding the purpose of education, teaching and learning practices, and assessment practices.

6.3.1 The purpose of education

How cultures and societies view the purpose of education influences how education systems develop, what is included and excluded in curricula, how universities are run, how teaching and learning occur in the classroom, and how student assessments are conducted. Biesta (2015) suggests that the purposes of education include dimensions of *"qualification, socialisation, and subjectification"* (p. 77). *"Qualification has to do with the transmission and acquisition of knowledge, skills and dispositions"* (Biesta, 2015, p. 77). Beginning from primary school, we attend formal education. We attend school daily to learn mathematics, languages, music, art, literature, and science. At the end of primary school, we move on to secondary school, where we continue our studies and receive a diploma upon completion. When we enter a university, it is different. We become specialized in the subjects we learn. For example, we may choose to study social science, so those courses will be our priority. We will receive a degree certificate upon completing a bachelor's level university program. We may continue to study for a master's or PhD degree, and after each course of study, we will receive a certificate that "proves" we have met the university's criteria and are qualified in a given area.

The next dimension of the purpose of education is socialization. *"Through education we also represent and initiate children and young people in traditions and ways of being and doing"* (Biesta, 2015, p. 77). An excellent example of how education teaches us socialization is to consider the behavior of young children. When young children are frustrated, angry, or confused, they sometimes act out. Imagine two children playing in a primary school physical education class. Ruby steals Charles' football. Charles becomes upset and kicks Ruby. The teacher sees the altercation and speaks to both children first about how stealing other people's belongings is wrong and secondly about how we can deal with conflict without resorting to physical violence. Through these kinds of lessons, some of which may be formal (for example, in moral education classes) or informal, as in the case of this example, students come to learn what is socially acceptable and inappropriate behavior.

According to Biesta (2015), education's final purpose is subjectification. This purpose prepares students to be active members of society and to make well-informed and responsible decisions about their lives (Biesta, 2020). It does not center around individualism but helps us place ourselves in the world in relation to others.

Contrasting essentialist descriptions

Education systems globally emphasize various purposes to varying degrees, influenced by economic development, cultural background, and historical context. In the context of Western education systems, some scholars have identified subjectification as important and labeled Western education systems *"mind oriented"* (Li, 2005, p. 191). According to scholars, this approach values and fosters skills like skepticism, independence, critical thinking, autonomy, and agency in students (Li, 2005). Historically, scholars have viewed qualification as the means to facilitate meaningful aspects of life rather than an end goal, with socialization occurring both within educational institutions and in the wider community, reflecting diverse cultural groups.

In contrast, Chinese educational systems have been described as *"virtue oriented"* by scholars, emphasizing virtues such as *"resolve, diligence, endurance of hardship, perseverance, and concentration"* (Li, 2005, p. 191). Scholars have often viewed qualifications as the pathway to students' stable and financially secure future.

Other possibilities

All students are concerned with qualifications, especially considering the economic downturn of the global economy. Although countries are recovering, living and housing costs still concern many students (World Bank, 2022). Higher education is viewed as one way to ensure a secure future economically. Global economic and job markets complicate education greatly because professors no longer educate students to contribute to one society and fulfill their country's financial needs. They are educating students to take positions in a globally competitive market, which requires similar qualifications from students and employees.

Socialization is a purpose of most education systems to maintain traditions and cultures, but how Western and Chinese universities implement socialization may differ. Western universities and professors may implicitly model desirable attitudes and behavior for students (Samuelson et al., 2015), while Chinese universities may prefer explicit instruction. Subjectification is similar, except in this case, Western universities tend to be more explicit and Chinese implicit in their teaching.

As the world becomes more economically and socially intertwined, the purposes of education are also becoming more equally adopted in educational institutions. Although the method and content of teaching are different, qualification, socialization, and subjectification are common purposes of education to prepare students for their future professional and social lives in a globalizing world.

6.3.2 How education is "done": Teaching and learning

Teaching styles usually fall into two categories: student/learner-centered or teacher-centered. In classrooms where student-centered learning is prioritized, *"the teacher...should lead from behind"* (Chase, 2017), and students' participation and engagement are considered crucial components of the teaching and learning process. Lave and Wenger (2007) suggested that in student-centered learning, *"there are strong goals for learning because learners, as peripheral participants, can develop a view of what the whole enterprise is about, and what there is to be learned"* (p. 22). There is also recognition that not all students prefer to learn or learn effectively in the same way. Gardner (1983) outlined different ways students learn best: visually, verbally, musically, logically, interpersonally, intrapersonally, naturalistically, and kinesthetically. In student-centered learning approaches, instructors try to discover how each of their students learns best and then use different teaching techniques and activities so that each student can learn concepts in their preferred style. Active learning in this type of classroom involves collaborative learning, experiential learning (learning by doing), cooperation, and developing communities of learning and inquiry. Teacher-centered approaches mean that the teacher designs his/her classes, considering their curriculum knowledge as essential for student academic success. In this case, *"a teacher...imparts knowledge and resolves doubts"* (Gu et al., 2017, p. 12). In these types of classrooms, the teacher is an authority figure who plays a critical role in their students' learning. The teacher performs most of the explanations given on topics, and the student's role is to listen and learn what is being said and taught. Students in this type of classroom take a more passive role in the learning process.

Contrasting essentialist descriptions

Scholarly research indicates that many Western educational institutions employ student-centered learning approaches to enhance critical thinking, knowledge creation, problem-solving abilities, and student autonomy. In these settings, students often engage actively with lecturers, challenging and developing new knowledge. According to Li (2005), *"personal curiosity, intrinsic enjoyment, and a disposition to challenge or question given knowledge accompany the learner throughout these processes"* (p. 191). This aligns with Clanton Harpine's (2015) observation that students tend to excel when driven by intrinsic motivation (pp. 87-107), a focus of many Western educational systems.

In a different context, some scholars, like Zhang (2021), have suggested that *"on a continuum of learner/teacher-centered pedagogy, classrooms in Chinese higher education tend to be more teacher-centered"* (p. 235). This approach is seen as effective in fostering subject knowledge acquisition.

Scholars suggest that students in such environments often respect educators by attentively following instructions, engaging in content memorization, and participating when prompted (Gu et al., 2017; Zhang, 2021). Li (2005) explains this respect as *"not mean[ing] blind acceptance of what is taught—rather, the idea of humility"* (p. 191) towards educators, who are regarded as highly respected members of society. While intrinsic motivation is highly valued, the role of extrinsic motivation is also recognized. For example, Liu et al. (2020) found that *"for students with low intrinsic motivation, ... the extrinsic motivation helped to improve academic performance"* (p. 584), suggesting a nuanced view of student motivation in educational settings.

Other possibilities

With the rise in globalization, multinational companies' global hiring practices have influenced education by identifying which skills are most valued. Universities have had to ensure that the desired skills are part of the curricula, thus helping their students compete with their international peers.

> As businesses and industries face a stronger competition in the marketplace, employers increasingly prefer hiring those graduates who possess the latest technical and soft skills that are necessary for the workplace. These skills include analytic thinking, collaboration, individual initiative, computer skills, and fluency in international languages
>
> (Chapman & Sarvi, 2017, p 33).

To meet the economic demand, universities worldwide have had to readjust their curricula, and instructors have had to readjust how they teach to foster the desired soft skills in their students. The influence of companies on education is not a regional issue; it is global, and every university system and country faces similar trends.

6.3.3 How education is "done": Assessment

Assessment is the term used by educators to describe how students' knowledge and learning are tested. There are two forms of assessment: formative assessment (assessment for learning) and summative assessment (assessment of learning). Formative assessment is feedback lecturers give students to improve student work and encourage further learning, but no grade is associated with it. In contrast, summative assessments are graded exams that may include feedback.

Contrasting essentialist descriptions

According to some scholars, Western assessment practices combine both formative and summative assessments (Northern Illinois University Faculty Development and Instructional Design Center, n.d.). Bloom's taxonomy comprises six levels, "*remembering, understanding, applying, analyzing, evaluating and creating*" (Chandio et al., 2016, p. 203), and is commonly used to assess students in formative and summative assessments. In the first level (knowledge), "*the teacher is attempting to determine whether the students can recognize and recall information*"; in the second level (comprehension), "*the teacher wants the students to be able to arrange or, in some way, organize information*"; in the third level (application), "*the teacher begins to use abstractions to describe particular ideas or situations*"; in the fourth level (analysis), "*the teacher begins to examine elements and the relationships between elements or the operating organizational principles undergirding an idea*"; in the fifth level (synthesis), "*the teacher is beginning to help students put conceptual elements or parts together in some new plan of operation or development of abstract relationships*"; and in the final level (evaluation) "*the teacher helps students understand the complexity of ideas so that they can recognize how concepts and facts are either logically consistent or illogically developed*" (Lasley, 2023, para 6). Understanding concepts and putting concepts together logically to form one's opinions or ideas or identifying, through critical thinking, how others' arguments are logical/illogical are viewed as skills that students should be able to have and put into practice. These skills are developed through critical essay writing and/or group/solo research projects. Students are unaware of their rank in the class.

According to some scholars, such as Chen et al. (2021), some universities in underdeveloped regions of China tend to prioritize summative assessment over formative because of "*insufficient support, improper dissemination and ineffective training at the meso-level and the instructors' limited assessment ability, large class sizes and student's resistance at the micro-level*" (p. 649). Standardized testing for student assessment includes questions with definite, prescribed answers and is usually conducted at regular intervals. Types of assessment include "*pop quizzes, unit tests, monthly tests, mid-terms tests, end-of-term tests, graduation exam, and entrance exams for junior/senior middle school and college*" (Gu et al., 2017, p. 36). Scholars point out that a great deal of importance is placed on preparing students for assessment, and educators may focus their teaching on exam-related content (Zhao, 2023). Students are often aware of their rank within the class.

Other possibilities

For Western countries, the rise in international competition has meant that national school systems are beginning to place a great deal of value on school performance and national ranking on international league tables such as The Program for International Student Assessment (PISA) tests, even though this type of testing is known to be inaccurate and unreliable (Berliner, 2020; Fernandez-Cano, 2016; Goldstein, 2017). Likewise, universities globally compete to gain "top 200" status in world rankings on lists such as Times Higher Education (Times Higher Education, n.d.). This trend of global education competition between countries and educational institutions has made assessment practices more competitive and standardized, focusing primarily on summative assessments worldwide.

Both formative and summative assessments are used in Western and Chinese education. In both contexts, lecturers give students feedback on their work (formative assessment) to ensure success during summative assessments. Although standardized exams in China are still commonly used, not all exams use the same format (Gu et al., 2017, p. 36). What type of assessments are given to students is also influenced by the class size (Chen et al., 2021).

6.4 Case Study Assignment

In Section 6.3, comparisons were made between Western and Chinese education based on the literature in terms of purposes of education, teaching and learning styles, and different types of assessment. Work in groups to discuss the following questions:

(1) Are the generalizations presented accurate?

(2) In your opinion, what is the purpose of education?

(3) In your university experience, what style of teaching and learning have you had, student or teacher-centered? Which do you prefer?

(4) What is your motivation for studying, intrinsic or extrinsic?

(5) What type of assessment is most important for your learning: formative or summative?

6.5 Chapter Summary

This chapter began by examining the nature of education through a discussion of formal and informal education and the necessity of comparative education as a sub-discipline of educational studies. Next, literature was introduced about different perspectives on the purposes of education and how different societies and cultures emphasize different purposes. How these ideas reflect real-world classroom practices regarding teaching and learning styles and assessment types were compared.

By understanding the concepts of essentialism, globalization, and convergence theory, we can recognize how problematic strict dichotomies are. We can also better understand people, societies, and education systems by considering other possibilities outside contrasting essentialist descriptions. We can identify our commonalities while still recognizing our differences. We can also understand why our differences exist.

References

Berliner, D. C. (2020). The implications of understanding that PISA is simply another standardized achievement test. In G. Fan & T. S. Popkewitz (Eds.), *Handbook of education policy studies: school/university, curriculum, and assessment* (Vol. 2, pp. 239-258). SpringerOpen. https://doi.org/10.1007/978-981-13-8343-4

Biesta, G. (2015). What is education for? On good education, teacher judgement, and educational professionalism. *European Journal of Education, 50*(1), 75-87. https://doi.org/10.1111/ejed.12109

Biesta, G. (2020). Risking ourselves in education: Qualification, socialization, and subjectification revisited. *Educational Theory, 70*(1), 89-104. https://doi.org/10.1111/edth.12411

Bray, M., Adamson, B., & Mason, M. (Eds.). (2014). *Comparative education research: Approaches and methods*. SpringerLink. https://doi.org/10.1007/978-3-319-05594-7

Cambridge Dictionary. (2023). Essentialism. In *Cambridge Dictionary*. Retrieved from https://dictionary.cambridge.org/dictionary/english/essentialism

Chandio, M. T., Pandhiani, S. M., & Iqbal, R. (2016). Bloom's taxonomy: Improving assessment and teaching-learning process. *Journal of Education and Educational Development, 3*(2), 203-221.

Chapman, D., & Sarvi, J. (2017). Widely recognized problems, controversial solutions: Issues and strategies for higher education development in east and southeast Asia. In K. H. Mok (Ed.). *Managing international connectivity, diversity of learning and changing labour markets: East Asian perspectives* (pp. 25-46). Springer. https://doi.org/10.1007/978-981-10-1736-0

Chase, B. (2017). An American special education teacher's reflections. In R. Maclean (Ed.), *Life in schools and classrooms: Past, present and future* (pp. 573-585). Springer. https://doi.org/10.1007/978-981-10-3654-5

Clanton Harpine, E. (2015). *Group-centered prevention in mental health: Theory, training, and practice.* Springer. https://doi.org/10.1007/978-3-319-19102-7

Chen, Q., Zhang, J., & Li, L. (2021). Problematising formative assessment in an undeveloped region of China: Voices from practitioners. *Educational Assessment, Evaluation, and Accountability, 33,* 649-673.

Confucius. (1861). The Analects [論語] (J. Legge, Trans.). Retrieved from https://ctext.org/analects

Fernandez-Cano, A. (2016). A methodological critique of the PISA evaluations. *Relieve, 22*(1), 1-16. https://dx.doi.org/10.7203/relieve.22.1.8806

Gardner, H. (1983). *Frames of mind: The theory of multiple intelligences.* Basic Books.

Giddens, A. (2002). *Runaway world.* Profile Books.

Goldstein, H. (2017). Measurement and evaluation issues with PISA. In L. Volante (Ed.), *The PISA effect on global educational governance.* Routledge. Retrieved from https://www.bristol.ac.uk/media-library/sites/cmm/migrated/documents/Measurement%20and%20Evaluation%20Issues%20with%20PISA.pdf

Gu, M., Ma, J., & Teng, J. (2017). *Portraits of Chinese schools.* Springer.

Jenkins, M. (2018). *Dialectic: From Hegel to Althusser. An introduction.* Lightning Source UK Ltd.

Kneissel, J., Huyssen, A., & Moore, J. (1974). The convergence theory: The debate in the federal Republic of Germany. *New German Critique,* (2), 16-27.

Kolb, D. A. (1984). *Experiential learning: Experience as the source of learning and development.* Prentice-Hall.

Lasley, T. J. (2023). Bloom's taxonomy. In *Encyclopedia Britannica.* Retrieved from https://www.britannica.com/topic/Blooms-taxonomy

Lave, J., & Wenger, E. (2007). Learning and pedagogy in communities of practice. In J. Leach & B. Moon (Eds.), *Learners and pedagogy* (pp. 21-33). Paul Chapman Publishing.

Li, J. (2005). Mind or virtue: Western and Chinese beliefs about learning. *Current Directions in Psychological Science, 14*(4), 190-194.

Liu, Y., Hau, K.-T., Liu, H., Wu, J., Wang, X., & Zheng, X. (2020). Multiplicative effect of intrinsic and extrinsic motivation on academic performance: A longitudinal study of Chinese students. *Journal of Personality, 88*(3), 584-595. https://doi.org/10.1111/jopy.12512

Manzon, M. (2011). *Comparative education: The construction of a field.* Springer.

Northern Illinois University Faculty Development and Instructional Design Center. (n.d.). Formative and summative assessment. Retrieved from https://www.niu.edu/citl/resources/guides/instructional-guide/formative-and-summative-assessment.shtml

Outhwaite, W. (2016). *Social theory: Ideas in profile.* Profile Books.

Samuelson, P. L., Jarvinen, M. J., Paulus, T. B., Church, I. M., Hardy, S. A., & Barrett, J. L. (2015). Implicit theories of intellectual virtues and vices: A focus on intellectual humility. *Journal of Positive Psychology, 10*(5), 389-406. https://doi.org/10.1080/17439760.2014.967802.

Times Higher Education. (n.d.). *Home.* Retrieved from https://www.timeshighereducation.com

University Alliance of the Silk Road (UASR). (n.d.). *Home.* Retrieved from http://uasr.xjtu.edu.cn

World Bank. (2022). *World Development Report 2022: Finance for an equitable recovery.* International Bank for Reconstruction and Development / The World Bank. https://www.worldbank.org

Zhang, B. (2021). A comparison between pedagogical approaches in UK and China. *Journal of Comparative & International Higher Education, 13*(5), 232-242. https://doi.org/10.32674/jcihe.v13i5.2629

Zhao, H. (2023). The influence of test-oriented teaching on Chinese students' long-term use of English. *International Journal of Education and Humanities, 6*(2), 123-128.

7

Comparing Cultures Through Visual Arts

Chen Dadi, Han Lu and Ge Dongmei

7.1 Concrete Experience

We begin this chapter with a cross-cultural talk between two painters in the 18th century China through two paintings of Chinese peonies (see Figures 7.1 & 7.2).[1]

Figure 7.1
Peonies by Giuseppe Castiglione (1688–1766)

Figure 7.2
Peony "Dancing Black Lion" by Zou Yigui (1688–1772)

---

1. The pictures in Chapters 7 and 8, unless indicated, are royalty-free images in the public domain without restriction under copyright or database law.

The peony is a flower symbolizing prosperity and fortune in Chinese culture. It is a popular subject in traditional Chinese paintings. The above paintings show two peonies in different colors, both elegant and beautiful. If we compare them, we will notice some differences in the details. The left one (Figure 7.1) is more lifelike than the right one (Figure 7.2) in that the stems and leaves have distinct outlines and shadows. It is more natural than the right one when we see one of the twigs boldly stretches and places itself before the blooming flower (thus showing the spatial relationship between the two); in the right painting, the flower is perfectly presented without any disturbance before it.

The left painting was painted by Giuseppe Castiglione (郎世宁), an Italian. In 1715, Castiglione arrived in China as a missionary. His skill as an artist was appreciated by the Emperor Qianlong and he became a painter in the court. Castiglione spent many years in the court painting various subjects, including the portraits of the Emperor and Empress. Castiglione combined European realistic technique with Chinese fine brushwork and expressions in his style (Geng, 2021).

However, when he started to show his works to Chinese viewers, his style was almost unacceptable. One of his Chinese colleagues in the court, Zou Yigui (邹一桂), who painted the right painting of peony, regarded the paintings by the westerners not to his liking:

> 西洋人善勾股法，故其绘画于阴阳、远近不差锱黍，所画人物、屋树皆有日影，其所用颜色与笔与中华绝异，布影由阔而狭，以三角量之，画宫室于墙壁，令人几欲走进。学者能参用一二，亦具醒法，但笔法全无，虽工亦匠，故不入画品。
>
> ——邹一桂《小山画谱》

Castiglione realized that to please his Chinese viewers he had to "unlearn" a lot of what he learnt in Italy. For example, Emperor Qianlong thought that shadows in a portrait looked like dirt on the face. Therefore, when Castiglione painted the emperor, the intensity of the light was reduced so that there was no shadow on the face. Castiglione influenced Qing court paintings in a short period. Other Chinese and European painters followed his footsteps and a new school of painting appeared, which combined Chinese and Western painting techniques. The influence of Western art on the Qing court paintings is particularly evident in the light, shade, perspective, as well as the priority given to recording contemporary events (Yang, et al., 2002; Yang, 2017). We can see this new cross-cultural style in the painting in Figure 7.1 when comparing with Zou's traditional painting in Figure 7.2.

The story is not over yet. One hundred years later, in the late 19th century Europe, artists were fascinated by the artistic pieces brought back by missionaries, businessmen, or soldiers from the East. European modernist painters, such as Claude Monet in France and Vincent van Gogh in the Netherlands, started to adopt elements from Asian cultures in their artistic creation. Monet painted his wife in a Japanese kimono holding a Japanese fan in her hand (Figure 7.3). Van Gogh was inspired by the perspective, compositions, outlines and colors in Japanese ukiyo-e prints and the use of colors in those pictures (Figure 7.4). New schools of art, such as Expressionism, abandoned the faithful depiction of the real physical world, and presented the world from a subjective perspective, changing it dramatically for emotional effect to evoke moods or inspire ideas. A thousand years after artistic styles began to diverge in China and the West (see Section 7.2.2), artists from the different cultures found inspirations in each other's artistic creation.

Figure 7.3

Madame Monet in kimono by Claude Monet (1840–1926) in 1876

Figure 7.4

Almond Flowers by Vincent van Gogh (1853–1890)

The conversation goes on. Today, when we walk into an art museum or gallery, it is not difficult to find modern paintings with recognizable elements of visual arts from various cultures. Artists all over the world are more and more proud of displaying artworks comprising elements of their cultural heritage. International art projects and events, such as UNESCO International Arts Education Week and the International Dunhuang Project (IDP), bring people together to communicate through artifacts, to promote cultural diversity by appreciating and preserving world artistic heritage, and to share inspirations for more creative artworks.

In this chapter, we compare the development of art in China and the West in the Reflective Observation, searching for keys to unlock the mystery behind such difference and collision in the Abstract Conceptualization, and looking for bridges to "cross" the border in the Active Experimentation.

Activity 7-1   Matteo Ricci (利玛窦, 1552-1610), an Italian priest who visited China during Ming Dynasty in 1582, was the first European invited by the Emperor to the Forbidden City. He noticed some differences between Chinese and Western paintings, e.g., no shadow on the faces in Chinese portraits.[1] Can you find another pair of Chinese and Western paintings that exhibit some differences? Can you point out the differences and explain them?

Activity 7-2   Castiglione was appointed by the Emperor to be in charge of designing the Western-Style palaces in the imperial gardens of the Old Summer Palace (圆明园). Ironically, the Palace was looted and destroyed in the war between Chinese and Western armies about 100 years after his death. How much do you know about the Old Summer Palace? Can you find out how Castiglione combined the Chinese and European styles in the design?

Activity 7-3   Wouldn't it be fun to recreate a famous painting (Western or Chinese) in your own way? You can use any material to recreate the painting or dress up as a character from the painting (you can invite your friends). You can find some inspirations in many examples online, e.g., "20 Modern Remakes of Famous Paintings" by

---

1. 据明代顾起元《客座赘语》所载，利玛窦曾说："中国画但画阳，不画阴，故看之人面躯正平，无凹凸相。吾国画兼阴与阳写之，故面有高下，而手臂皆轮圆耳，凡人之面，正迎阳，则皆明而白，若侧立，则向明一边者白，其不向明一边者，眼耳鼻口凹处皆有暗相。吾国之写像者解此法，用之故能使画像与生人无异也。"

Dovas on bordedpanda.com.

7.2 Reflective Observation

Visual arts provide us delight and impact through various forms and styles. Though the origins of art were quite similar in various world cultures, along with the development of the cultures, visual arts in the East and West diverged and became distinctive. In the following sections, we trace back thousands of years to see the similar origins of visual arts in China and the West, as well as the process of their divergence and the formation of their distinctive features.

7.2.1 The similar origins

Art originated from the symbols for natural objects, like how all the languages develop. With simple strokes, outlines, and "carton" figures, early paintings imitated the simple and familiar objects in life, or strange and mysterious creatures in nature. These paintings very often shared the same function as language, i.e., recording and representing what happened in the real world. European prehistoric art appeared earlier than Chinese art (see the examples in Figures 7.5 and 7.6). We find some common characteristics of cave paintings or female statuettes in both cultures, such as the functions of art, the use of natural colors, the sites of painting and types of statuettes, etc.

Figure 7.5
Cave paintings at Lascaux

There are some 2,000 figurative pictures in total, including 900 animal forms and many abstract images and symbols. The appearance of a plot in the painting indicates people were able to tell a story of hunting through painting. The age of the paintings is estimated at around 17,000 years.

Figure 7.6
Painting from Mount Helan

Mount Helan is in Ningxia Hui Autonomous Region, Northwest China. The Nomads' carvings were probably finished between 4,000 and 10,000 years ago, which illustrate mainly the animals and the hunting of big game.

It can be seen from the artifacts of early times that people in China and the West lived and created art works in similar ways. Men and women survived by hunting animals, fishing, and collecting natural fruits, herbs and plants. Nature provided them not only water, food and warmth, but also pleasure and terror. All these things were recorded in paintings as hope of life or awe of nature. Furthermore, since fertility is critical to the survival of all species on the planet, the female statuettes, perhaps as the symbols of the Goddess of Birth that worshiped by people all around the prehistoric world, were so popular in both cultures (see the examples in Figures 7.7 and 7.8).

Figure 7.7
The Venus of Willendorf

This statuette of a female figure estimated to have been made between 24,000 and 22,000 BCE.

Figure 7.8
Goddess of Hongshan

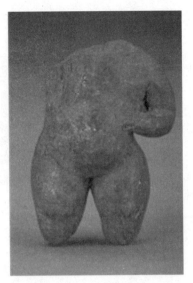

This pottery statuette of a pregnant woman was unearthed at the Hongshan Culture Site of Dongshanzui, Liaoning Province, Northeast China. The statuette can be compared to the Paleolithic Venus Figurines found in Europe.

7.2.2 The divergence between East and West

As the ancient cultures developed, the visual arts in different cultures became more and more distinct with their own characteristics. In Europe, painting and sculptures emphasized more the resemblance to reality, while in China, art works became more and more symbolic, and they embodied the ideals and aspirations of the artists. In the following, we review the development of visual arts from Bronze Age to Middle Ages to see how visual arts diverged in different cultures.

Bronze Age

The Bronze Age began at different times in Europe and China. In Greece, as represented by the Aegean civilization, it began around 3000 BCE, while in China, as represented by Shang and Zhou dynasties, it began around 1600 BCE. We see divergence in this period between European and Chinese cultures, as it is demonstrated in visual arts.

In ancient Greece, visual arts were stimulated by democracy, flourishing economy, philosophical ideas of artistic creation, and some of the contemporary events such as the Olympics. Sculptures in Aegean civilization were characterized as masks or small-size figures for ornament, inspired mainly by religion and myths (see Figure 7.9). While in China, the establishment of feudalism and the influence of Confucianism cast the molds for art works, like types and patterns symbolizing social codes, ranks and social status, etc. The chaos of wars hindered the development of economy and visual art, making art works more fit for practical use. The artifacts in Shang and Zhou dynasties were more utilitarian. Some were made for practical use in ordinary life, and other ones for ceremonies (see Figure 7.10).

Figure 7.9

The "Mask of Agamemnon"

The artifact is a funeral mask hewn in gold. The founder Heinrich Schliemann in 1876 believed that he had discovered the body of the legendary Greek leader Agamemnon, but modern archaeological research suggests that the mask is from 1550–1500 BCE (earlier than the life of Agamemnon).

Figure 7.10

Houmuwu square cauldron (后母戊鼎)

It was casted in the late Shang Dynasty (1600–1046 BCE) presumably by the king of Shang to carry out rituals for his mother Fuhao (妇好). It is grandiose and elegant with a beautiful design and various symbols (e.g., animal or human face, dragon, tiger, clouds and thunder), showing a superb level of casting, and is the largest Shang ritual bronze vessel found to date (Yu, 2024; Photo by Mlogic/CC-BY-SA-3.0).

The visual arts of ancient Greece have influenced enormously the cultures of many countries all over the world, particularly in the field of European sculpture and architecture. In the West, the art of the Roman Empire was largely derived from Greek models. In the East, Alexander the Great's conquests initiated several centuries of exchange among Greek, Central Asian, and Indian cultures, resulting in the Greco-Buddhist art which was spreaded along the Silk Road to Japan and China (Gombrich E. H. & Gombrich, L., 2023). Later ideas about fine arts in Europe were developed from Mimesis (see 7.3 for the details). Following the Renaissance in Europe, the humanist aesthetics and the high technical standards of Greek art inspired generations of European artists. For example, art forms in the Classic Period of Ancient Greece greatly influenced the Classic Art in the 17th Century and the Neo-Classic Art in the 19th Century.

Visual arts in the Zhou Dynasty were much influenced by Confucianism. Heaven was seen as an approving or disapproving instance; the compound of buildings, hierarchical social system, and the bureaucratic state became parts of the traditional and unified Chinese culture, as reflected in the symbols and patterns on the bronze vessels and other artistic works.

Ancient Rome and Qin and Han dynasties

Both Ancient Rome in the West and Qin and Han Dynasties in the East were established and became prosperous on the basis of military conquests, which made the art of these two periods similar in boasting military victories and power. The purpose of visual arts in the period was to preach to the public the power of the rulers (see the examples in Figures 7.11 and 7.12).

Figure 7.11
Arch of Constantine

The Arch celebrated the victory of Constantine, and conveyed the theme of praising the emperor, both in battle and in his civilian duties.

Figure 7.12
Terracotta Army

There are over 6,000 terra cotta warriors and horses in Pit 1 near Qin Shihuang's Mausoleum. They are marshaled into a well-organized battle array protecting the emperor in his afterlife.

Due to the different philosophic views on nature, artistic creation became different in the two cultures. Roman artists tended to represent the real images of people and beautify them by highly rationalized and idealized proportion, such as the giant sculptures of Roman rulers, and lifelike human figures in sculptures. Their portrait sculptures were known for the distinctive facial expressions (see the example in Figure 7.13). Chinese artists adopted symbolized ways to present the ideas, and neglect some of the trivial details. Taking the sculpture *Horse Treads on a Hun* for example (see Figure 7.14), the figure of the horse and the Hun were carved according to the natural

Figure 7.13
Series of ancient Roman portrait sculptures

From left to right: Agrippa (Second part of the 1st century CE), Emperor Caracalla (c. 188–217), Colossus of Constantine (c. 312-315).

Figure 7.14

Horse Treads on a Hun (马踏匈奴)

The stone carving was found in front of Huo Qubing's tomb. Majestically, the horse is holding its head proudly erect, symbolizing the heroic posture of the General and his brave army, while under the horse's feet is the figure of an old and defeated Hun slave owner (Photo from Sina.com.cn).

shape of the stone instead of real images of horses and men. Details of real objects, such as light and shade, exact sizes of things and special relationship among them, were neglected or reduced. Such simplicity and exaggeration allowed the artists to highlight the theme and their feelings. This trend of seeing and depicting things from a subjective view reflected the Chinese philosophical idea of "the unity of heaven and human"(天人合一).

7.2.3 Distinctive styles of Chinese and Western visual arts

We have seen in the previous section the divergence between the Chinese and Western visual arts. In later eras, visual arts continued to develop, not only in the skills and techniques, but also in the approaches and art theories. Artistic creation became more and more a conscious and individualized expression, rather than recording historical events, demonstrating religious ideas, satisfying the patrons, or imitation and repetition of fashionable models.

From the Middle Ages through the Renaissance, painters worked for churches and wealthy aristocracies, making a living by the support of their patrons. Their principles of proportion, light, color and symbolism in arts were formed in the realm of the popular religious belief. The mosaic *Empress Theodora and Retinue* (Figure 7.15), for example, is one of the most famous mosaics in the Byzantine time. It is one of the two panels facing the altar from opposite sides in the apse of San Vitale, a church in an Italian coastal town called Ravenna, the last capital of the West Roman Empire and the new capital of the East Roman Empire in the late 5th and early 6th century. The Roman Empire collapsed, and Christianity was adopted as an official religion in the Empire. The church of San Vitale was begun in 526 and consecrated in 547, when the ambitious Emperor Justinian asserted his power in Italy after the Byzantine conquest, and wished to restore the glory of the Roman Empire not only by military force, but also by religious power. In another painting, he was standing there with twelve attendants, simulating Jesus and his twelve followers, and claiming his ultimate and even permanent power in earthly life. The Empress Theodora (c. 500–548), the wife of Emperor Justinian, accompanied by seven ladies of the court and two men, was placed slightly off center in the mosaic, and was crowned with a halo. The prominent position of Theodora's mosaic shows her status as co-regent. Her attire is richly embellished with jewels. Strings of iridescent pearls (at that time believed to have power in preventing sickness) drip from her extravagant crown. The modeling of her face and clothing is achieved through the use of color, a characteristically Byzantine stylistic feature (e.g., her upper lip which is darker than the lower lip, and the deeply shaded folds of her robes). Light, as expounded by the abundance of gold backgrounds and their reflected surfaces, is symbolic of Christ's self-proclaimed role as "light of the world". In the mosaic pictures describing their attendance of the religious service, the figures face towards the audience, with stern faces and looks, and wine jar in the hands of the Emperor, and challis in the hands of the Empress, showing clearly not only their piety in faith, but also the social and political background of the 6th century Europe.

Figure 7.15
Mosaic of Theodora and Retinue

(Photo by Petar Milošević/CC BY-SA, Wikipedia)

While in China, painting and sculpture also played an important role in life, demonstrating not only religious concepts (as seen in Buddhist, Taoist, and Confucian temples and the residence of the believers), but also the idea of royal power, the wish of blessed fortune, the inner comfort of reclusion, and aesthetic sentiment.

Academic painters（院体派画家）from the Han (202 BCE–220 CE) to the Tang (618–907) dynasties mainly painted human figure. Much of what we know of early Chinese figure painting came from burial sites, where paintings were preserved on silk banners, lacquered objects and tomb walls. Many early tomb paintings were meant to protect the dead or help their souls get to paradise. Others illustrated the teachings of Confucius, or showed scenes of daily life.

Zhou Fang's *Ladies with Head-pinned Flowers* (Figure 7.16) in the late 8th century can be taken as a good example to see the social life at that time. Zhou Fang was one of the most important portrait painters in the mid-Tang Dynasty. The painting depicted the leisurely and carefree life of court ladies in the Tang Dynasty—the five ladies wearing magnificent clothes with a maid, strolling in the flower garden. The early period of the Tang Empire witnessed the peace and prosperity brought by the wise political and economic policies. Cultural integration, flexible international relations and flourishing foreign trade profited the businessmen and the Empire. Chang'an, the capital of the empire, also became a world cultural and economic center. Women enjoyed much freedom. Fuller figures were regarded as beautiful, and innovative dresses were encouraged and admired. Women were appointed as officials in the court, and were even allowed to divorce their husbands. The ladies portrayed in the painting were regarded as typical fashionable beauties at that time, with their hair like a cloud and pinned with Chinese peony, which has always been regarded as a symbol of prosperity and nobility till today. Their dresses were finely made in a sharp red color, one of the popular colors in the Tang Dynasty. The transparent brown gowns added elegance to the dresses and the colors went very well with the warm tune. Both the gowns and the dresses were made of silk, with delicate patterns on them, showing to the audience the advanced textile industry and the excellent skill of the tailors. The wide open collar allowed more femininity to be revealed and made the ladies more attractive. The loose shape of the dresses not only covered any imperfection of their figures, but also made them as graceful as fairies when walking. In the Tang Dynasty, Taoism was favored by the emperors and empresses. Such a popular trend obviously influenced fashion. Meanwhile, in many Buddhist paintings, goddesses were modeled after imperial court ladies, a development that indicated the trend of religious painting as becoming more realistic. The style of such paintings also became a model in later academic paintings.

Figure 7.16
Ladies with Head-pinned Flowers (《簪花仕女图》) by Zhou Fang (周昉)

Parallel to the development of decorative paintings by professional painters, known as *Academic paintings* (院体画), a new kind of painting by amateur painters such as scholars and officials came into being since Jin and Six dynasties, and fully developed during the Tang and Song dynasties, which is latter known as *Literati painting* (文人画). The *Literati painting* was considered as a way through which the Confucian *Jun Zi* (君子) or a noble man expressed his ethical personality, in much the same way as he wrote poetry. It was much less concerned with technical showiness. Instead, they preferred plain ink paintings, sometimes with minimal color, laying more emphasis on the idea that the style with which a painter controlled his brush and conveyed his inner thought and character—brushstrokes were seen as expressions of the spirit. That is why the "amateur" ink literati paintings are regarded as the highest form of art in China (Eno, 2015).

How did *Literati paintings* come into being? During the wars in the Tang and Song dynasties, many literary men were forced to leave their homes and lost opportunity to participate in the imperial exams for selecting officials. They were sad about their misfortunes and effects of this devastating upheaval were apparent in Song paintings; the misty and ethereal landscapes sometimes reflected conflicting emotions of regret, distress, and anxiety. The time from the Five Dynasties period to the Northern Song period (960–1127) is known as the "great age of Chinese landscape paintings". In the north, artists such as Jing Hao (荆浩), Fan Kuan (范宽) and Guo Xi (郭熙) painted pictures of towering mountains, using strong black lines, ink wash, and sharp, dotted brushstrokes to suggest rough stone (see the example in Figure 7.17). In the south, Dong Yuan (董源),

Ju Ran (巨然) and other artists painted the rolling hills and winding rivers of their native countryside in peaceful scenes with softer and rubbed brushwork. These two kinds of scenes and techniques became the classical styles of Chinese landscape paintings.

Figure 7.17
Snow Mountains by Guo Xi

This piece shows a scene of a deep and serene mountain valley covered with snow and several old trees struggling to survive on precipitous cliffs. It is a masterpiece of Guo Xi by using light ink and magnificent composition to express his open and high artistic conception.

The most obvious difference we see from this period is the establishment of various principles for artistic creation (see Section 7.3). When Western painters emphasized idealized proportion, lifelike light and shadow and religious symbols, Chinese artists regarded vitality inside the painting more important than similarity to the details of painted objects. The appearance of

Literati paintings in China, as a highly expressive form, opened a new field in world art history. The content and skills began to be used as means to convey the happiness, sorrow, frustrations and ambitions of the artists, illustrating perfectly through landscapes the Confucius ideal of noble men.

With the different principles, visual art developed on different tracks in China and Europe. In Europe, paintings and sculptures became more lavish and more lifelike, paving the way for the styles in Renaissance. In China, the art forms of academic and literati paintings became more distinct in style and left many works for later artists to imitate and to create.

We also see the important role of religions in the development of Chinese and European visual arts in this period. What people did in Europe to decorate churches and altars by paintings and sculptures was almost the same as people did in China to Buddhist temples and grottos. We may find differences in the places where they built churches, temples or grottos with different materials, structures and decorations at different places of the buildings. But the functions of such decorations were the same, i.e., to illustrate the religious teachings and make people feel reverent and respectful. Religions influenced the ideas of artistic creation as well, from the criteria people followed in paintings, to the theme and subject matters of the paintings and sculptures. That is why we also call the period "religious times".

The following periods of Renaissance and the Ming Dynasty saw great cultural movements in both Europe and China. The styles of European and Chinese visual arts became as distinct as the difference between Saint Peter's Basilica and the Forbidden City (now the Palace Museum). These are the periods when the most representative types of classic visual arts, such as oil paintings in Europe and paintings in China, became mature.

The differences can be illustrated by two examples from the two kinds of paintings to demonstrate the differences between Chinese and Western classic paintings, Da Vinci's *Mona Lisa* (Figure 7.18), and Tang Yin's *Court Ladies of the Former Shu* (Figure 7.19). The difference we notice first might be in the spatial relationship between the subject matters, the ladies, and the background. Tang Yin adopted oblique projection to show the relative positions of the women, instead of perspective.[1] We can figure out the positions of the ladies by the distances among them and to the audience. However, there is no detail of the background except the light brown color.

---

1. Perspective in painting means the art of drawing solid objects on a two-dimensional surface so as to give the right impression of their height, width, depth, and position in relation to each other.

The scene can be located anywhere, in the courtyard, the palace, or the garden. The painting looks quite flat, or as Charles Lamb saw it, floating about and unrestricted by any element.[1]

Figure 7.18
Mona Lisa by Leonardo da Vinci (1452–1519)

Figure 7.19
Court Ladies of the Former Shu (《王蜀宫妓图》) by Tang Yin (唐寅)

---

1. " ... men and women float about, uncircumscribed by any element, in that world before perspective ... ", from the 19th century English writer Charles Lamb's (1775–1834) famous essay "Old China".

In the painting of *Mona Lisa*, Da Vinci used one-point and aerial perspective.[1] The landscape in the background becomes vague and smaller, showing the spatial relationship caused by distance. The more distinct description of light and shadow over the figure of Mona Lisa makes us feel that she was portrayed right in front of us against the landscape in the distance, as in real life. Thanks to the development of autopsy and optics, painters were able to make vivid portraits. The distinction between rational thinking in the West and emotional thinking in China can be seen in developing and using different painting techniques. In addition, perceptions in cultures can also decide on how people make artworks. In *Court Ladies of the Former Shu*, for example, we can barely trace the light from right above by the intensity of folds on women's gowns on the opposite side. In traditional Chinese culture, too much shadow in painting is sinister and ugly,[2] and too much details bore the name ostentatious craft.[3]

Such a difference also illustrates another big difference between Chinese and Western paintings in that traditional Chinese painters followed subjective feelings and impressions of the scene. They would neglect any elements that may cause distraction in the painting. For example, in most portraits, there is a blank in the background. The Western painters, however, emphasized the representation of reality, or truth, following the classic theory of Mimesis. They would carefully choose a background and put the subject harmoniously in it, rather than total negligence.

The third difference in technique might be the outlines. In Tang Yin's painting, the subjects are defined by imagined outlines with distinct thin lines of strokes (which reminds us of the fact that the Chinese character for drawing, Huà (画), originated from the marking of boundaries), while *Mona Lisa* is painted with natural shadows closer to reality.

The material of painting is another difference. The left is painted by colored ink, the same kind of black ink as used in Chinese calligraphy. Actually, calligraphy and painting are considered to have developed from the same origin in China. The Western painters tend to use various colors to depict the real scene or effect. Oil was adopted in painting a long time ago and later in the 15th century became an important material for painting on canvas. Da Vinci used oil on poplar, a new material he developed on the basis of the popular oil paint.

---

1. Aerial perspective refers to the technique of representing more distant objects as fainter and smaller.
2. See Princess Leling's memoir about Empress Dowager Cixi, *Two Years in the Forbidden City*, and Shi and Zhang (2011).
3. Ostentatious craft: the skills adopted only to impress or attract notice.

The models in the two paintings look different, too, in their poses, eye contact, dresses, costume, hairstyle, etc., which reflect the fashion and culture at that time. The list of differences can go on like this for pages, but one thing is in common between the two, that the ladies in both the paintings are peaceful, beautiful, and elegant. Though the models in paintings have changed for countless times, the techniques remained for centuries and became the classic examples for later generations to follow. Such achievement also prepared the foundation for later innovations; until today, the modern painters still start from the imitation of classical paintings before they learn the ways to express themselves in their own ways. In the following section, we discuss further how the diverged ideas towards visual arts in China and the West become the inherited treasury of creativity for all mankind.

7.3 Abstract Conceptualization

In the above review, it is obvious that the origin, divergence and the development of distinctive styles of visual arts in China and the West always bond with the development of cultures. What is the relationship between visual art and culture? How did or will the ideas and styles of visual arts diverge, merge and evolve?

7.3.1 Visual arts as cultural products

If you plan to travel in Europe, Prague is a city you must visit. The historical center of the city, including the famous Prague Castle, Charles Bridge, Old Town Square, etc., has been listed in the UNESCO list of World Heritage Sites. You must be amazed by the architectures containing various styles from Romanesque, Gothic, Renaissance, Baroque, Rococo, etc., to Neo-Renaissance, Neo-Classical and even ultra-modern, and they are so beautifully combined. If you ask people who know the history of the city, they will tell you how simple it was to make it, i.e., by just following the trend. The city was destroyed several times in the past wars and riots. To save the budget and keep their cultural heritages in the reconstruction, people would rather rehabilitate the buildings instead of rebuilding them. During the rehabilitation, the architects and artists or even the construction workers, would integrate some of the most up-to-date designs and styles into the work. Guess what? It works.

Visual art is regarded as one of the cultural products (Holliday, 2011). It is the most visible and audible part in Schein's (1984) levels of culture and their interaction (see 1.3.1), and grouped into the Symbols and placed at the most outer and superficial layer in the "onion" model of culture by Hofstede et al. (2010) (see Figure 7.20). Paintings, sculptures, architecture and various artifacts are carriers of meanings shared by people in the culture, and can be easily developed, updated, spread, and imitated by them. As part of the Practices in the model, artworks, artistic creation and performances are visible to the "outsiders" (*ibid*). That's the secret of beauty in Prague, as well as in many similar historical towns and cities worldwide. In communication across cultures, visual arts are the most convenient parts of a culture that can be introduced and shared with people from another culture. You can find that the cities with the most various architectures are often the ones with a large population of immigrants. Other examples can be found in the variety of art exhibitions, performances and events in cross-cultural communication activities.

Figure 7.20
Manifestations of culture at different levels

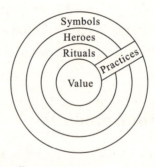

(Adapted from Hofstede et al., 2010, p. 8)

7.3.2 Artists, aesthetics and cultures

Right below the Symbols in the culture level model is the level of Heroes, who are the models for behavior in a culture (Hofstede et al., 2010). The philosophers in ancient Greece and China established different ideas about artistic creation. Representing reality was emphasized since Aristotle, demanded in Christian art, and revived in Renaissance; unification of human and nature was advocated in the literature of Confucianism, Taoism, and Buddhism in China. Influenced by mainstream culture values, philosophers and artists developed aesthetics, or the theory of beauty.

For example, the Ancient Greek philosopher Plato (427–347) considered that the art of painting is designed to be an imitation of appearance in reality. Thus came the original idea of mimesis which governed the art creation in

Europe for centuries. Plato also considered that beautiful objects incorporated proportion, harmony, and unity among their parts. Similar idea was proposed by Aristotle as well, who believed that the universal elements of beauty were order, symmetry and definiteness.

Such aesthetic approaches were further developed in the Middle Ages. Medieval aesthetics emphasized the symbolism of proportion and the effects of light and color. The artisans at that time often adopted symbolism which derived from a particular view of the world, i.e., the universe revealed God, its author or creator, through its beauty. They discovered certain pitches and proportions to be more pleasing to people than others, and these discoveries were propagated in the middle ages. To the medieval artisans, the effects of light became more important, particularly in architecture, and they frequently associated light with their theories of color. Light and color affected the thoughts of medieval thinkers on certain characteristics of beauty, such as radiance and clarity.

Later in the Renaissance, a group of artists including Leonardo da Vinci (1452–1519) and Michelangelo (1475–1564) became very influential through their works commissioned by the powerful nobles and churches. Leonardo da Vinci, for example, recorded in his Notebook his theories about composition and light. The "Old Masters" like him were often followed by apprentices, just as those craftsmen in other businesses, and those apprentices helped to spread the influences of their artistic styles and aesthetic ideas.

Aesthetics became the independent philosophy of art in the 18th century. Modern philosophers and art critics focus not only on the creation of beauty but also on the appreciation and judgment of it. John Ruskin (1819–1900) in the Victorian Britain, for example, defined painting or art in general is a noble and expressive language and the vehicle of thought (Ruskin, 1903), while the German philosopher Immanuel Kant (1724–1804) considered the judgments of beauty are not only sensory and emotional but also intellectual, because the judgments would involve our capacities of reflective contemplation (Kant, 1914). Another German philosopher Hegel (1770–1831) regards art as the first stage where the absolute spirit (he considered culture as a matter of "absolute spirit" manifesting itself) manifests directly and is immediately perceived by our senses. The idea resembles the cultural level model of Hofstede et al. (2010) which places art in the outer layer of Symbols. Aesthetics today continues to explore the mystery of beauty and becomes connected to not only philosophy, literature, etc., but also many other disciplines such as psychology, mathematics and information science.

Similar to the Ancient Greek thinkers, Chinese philosophers combined their definitions of art and beauty in their philosophical ideas. Confucius emphasized the unity of beauty and kindness as well as the pragmatic function of art in perfecting human nature and etiquette. Zhuangzi considered that the true beauty should not be defined by our sensory satisfaction. Instead, it manifests itself only in truth or Tao (道).

In the theories of painting developed by Chinese artists such as Gu Kaizhi (顾恺之, 348-405) and Xie He (谢赫), various techniques were summarized for all types of the paintings. Gu Kaizhi considered the portraits as the most difficult among all categories of paintings and explained how specific techniques could be used in portraying various characters from court ladies to drunkards. He wrote that the eyes were the spirit and most decisive factor of a successful portrait, more important than the clothes and the appearances. Xie He in the 6th century summarized the Six Principles of Painting (绘画六法), i.e.,

(1) *Spirit Resonance* (气韵生动), or the overall energy or vitality of the painting (as if everything in the painting is alive).

(2) *Bone Method* (骨法用笔), or the way of using the brush. This refers not only to texture and brush stroke, but also to the close link between handwriting and personality.

(3) *Correspondence to the Object* (应物象形), or the depicting of form, which would include shape and line.

(4) *Suitability to Type* (随类赋彩), or the application of color, including layers, value and tone.

(5) *Division and Planning* (经营位置), or placing and arrangement, should correspond to composition, space and depth.

(6) *Transmission by Copying* (传移模写), or the copying of models, not only from life but also the works of antiquity.

Though these principles were written some 1,600 years ago and referred previously only as principles in appreciating ancient paintings, art critics and painters who appreciate or practice traditional Chinese paintings today still abide by them. In these principles, we can see not only the painting skills, but also the ideas about fine art. Vitality transmitted from the artists into the work, rather than lifelike imitation of reality, was highlighted as the most important criteria for artistic creation. The colors and shapes should be suitable, rather than exactly faithful, to the objects. Placing and arrangement of objects were decided by the painters, rather than exact measurement of the real things. Artists can copy models not only from life, but also from the works of ancient times. None of these principles is compatible with what we see in the medieval art principles of Western cultures. Now, we probably can understand why Zou Yigui couldn't appreciate the Western paintings.

On the one hand, these principles set the tone for the development of Chinese paintings. Similar to the characteristics of communication in a high-context culture, Chinese paintings become more and more abstract, obscure and context-dependent. The artworks, especially the *Literati paintings*, often require enough contextual information to decipher. Some parts of the information become widely acknowledged symbolism, such as the peonies standing for prosperity, pine trees standing for long life, lonely women showing the languishing of demoted or discharged officials, and fishing or farming hermits showing the same as lonely women or carefree time in exile, etc. For the other parts of the information, the painters have to write some words or a poem to help the audience understand the prospect (意境), which makes it even harder for non-native speakers of Chinese language to understand or appreciate it.

On the other hand, however, these principles freed artists from the strict copying of real objects or events. A case in point might be the later more carefree skills in *Literati paintings*, as represented by "sketching thought" style (写意画). The inner energy or feelings transmitted through the work were regarded as more important than real size and color of the objects painted. The similar subjective perspective of artistic creation, about 1,500 years later, inspired Modernist artists in Europe.

7.3.3 Arts across cultures

Two hundred years later than Castiglione's arrival in the Forbidden City, when Western cultures "invaded" China, there was still disputes among Chinese artists about the difference in Chinese and Western styles of art. One group of the artists, like Pan Tianshou (潘天寿,1897–1971), Li Shutong (李叔同, 1880–1942), etc., still insisted that the different styles would never be reconciled. For example, Pan (2019) pointed out that the foundation of oriental painting is in philosophy while the foundation of western painting is in science. He believed that they are fundamentally in opposite directions. The other group of Chinese artists began to search for a way to combine the merits of both Chinese and Western styles. Xu Beihong (徐悲鸿, 1895–1953), for example, was one of the first Chinese artists to articulate the need for artistic expressions at the beginning of the 20th century. He was also regarded as one of the first to create monumental oil paintings with epic Chinese themes—a show of his high proficiency in an essential Western art technique. He proposed the "New Seven Laws" for paintings as a creative extension from Xie He's Six Principles but combined the latter with his own view for modern painting. Other Chinese painters started to study the techniques of Western artists shortly after the time when Van Gogh and Claude Monet followed their curiosity to explore Eastern arts and cultures. In different spaces but at almost the same time, Western and Eastern artists searched for the possibilities of combining different painting techniques. Zhang Daqian (张大千, 1899–1983) created a unique style of landscape painting when he was in Europe in the 1950s. His style was derived from the "broken-ink" techniques of random splashing and soaking used by Tang Dynasty artists, but it seems more likely that his encounter with Western abstract art encouraged him to carry further the Japanese technique of splashed colors that he had used in earlier works.

Art has no borders in the globalized era, especially when cross-cultural communication becomes a routine practice for people and when a common basis is acknowledged for appreciating, comparing and discussing arts and aesthetics. The contemporary philosopher Denis Dutton (1944–2010) identified 12 core items which can be found in arts across cultures and across times, i.e.,

(1) *Direct pleasure*. Visual arts or any other forms of arts are valued as the sources of immediate experiential pleasure in themselves, and not as useful in producing something else. Such aesthetic enjoyment is often said to be for its own sake.

(2) *Skill and virtuosity*. The making of the object requires and demonstrates the exercise of specialized skills. Such technical artistic skills can be acquired, like painting or sculpting, and recognized and universally admired by people.

(3) *Style*. Objects in all art forms are made in recognizable styles, according to rules of form, composition, or expression. Style provides a stable, predictable, and standard background against which artists may create elements of novelty and expressive surprise.

(4) *Novelty and creativity*. Art is valued, and appreciated, for its novelty, creativity, originality and capacity to surprise its audience.

(5) *Criticism*. All artistic forms exist alongside some kind of critical language of judgment, appreciation and elaboration.

(6) *Representation*. Art objects represent or imitate real and imaginary aspects of the world.

(7) *Special focus*. Works of art are set aside from ordinary life, making a separate and dramatic focus experience.

(8) *Expressive individuality*. It is possible to express individual personality in art practices.

(9) *Emotional saturation*. The represented content of art provokes emotions through the experience of works, e.g., pathos of a scene portrayed in a painting.

(10) *Intellectual challenge*. Works of art tend to be designed to utilize a combined variety of human perceptual and intellectual capacities.

(11) *Art traditions and institutions*. Art objects and performances are created and to a degree given significance by their place in the history and traditions of their art.

(12) *Imaginative experience*. Objects of art essentially provide an imaginative experience for both producers and audiences. For example, a marble carving may realistically represent an animal, but as a work of sculptural art it becomes an imaginative object (Dutton, 2009, pp. 45–53).

7.4 Active Experimentation

In this section, we invite you to join a pleasant experience of appreciating and promoting art works.

Activity 7-4 We have introduced to you in the previous section a list of 12 core items of arts proposed by Dutton (2009). In his book *What to listen for in Music,* Aaron Copland (2011) broke up the listening process into some component parts. According to his analysis, people all listen to music on three separate planes, i.e., sensuous plane, expressive plane and sheerly musical plane. We can do that in appreciating visual arts as well.

Step 1 Let's read the following excerpts from his book and compare his idea about the three planes with Dutton's 12 items in the appreciation of paintings. Think about this question: Which item(s) summarized by Dutton (2009) are similar to Copland's (2011) three planes of appreciating music? Can you explain the similarities from the perspective of art as a cultural product?

What to Listen for in Music

We all listen to music according to our separate capacities. But, for the sake of analysis, the whole listening process may become clearer if we break it up into its component parts, so to speak. In a certain sense we all listen to music on three separate planes. For lack of a better terminology, one might name these: (1) the sensuous plane, (2) the expressive plane, (3) the sheerly musical plane. The only advantage to be gained from mechanically splitting up the listening process into these hypothetical planes is the clearer view to be had of the way in which we listen.

The simplest way of listening to music is to listen for the sheer pleasure of the musical sound itself. That is the sensuous plane. It is the plane on which we hear music without thinking, without considering it in any way. One turns on the radio while doing something else and absent-mindedly bathes in the sound. A kind of brainless but attractive state of mind is engendered by the mere sound appeal of the music. The surprising thing is that many people who consider themselves qualified music lovers abuse that plane in listening. They go to concerts in order to lose themselves. They use music as a consolation or an escape. They enter an ideal world where one doesn't have to think of the realities of everyday life. The sensuous plane is an important one in music, a very important one, but it does not constitute the whole story.

The second plane on which music exists is what I have called the expressive one. Heaven knows it is difficult enough to say precisely what it is that a piece of music means, to say it definitely, to say it finally so that everyone is satisfied with your explanation. But that should not lead one to the other extreme of denying to music the right to be "expressive". My own belief is that all music has an expressive power, some more and some less, but that all music has a certain meaning behind the notes and that the meaning behind the notes constitutes, after all, what the piece is saying, what the piece is about. Let us suppose that you are fortunate and can describe to your own satisfaction in so many words the exact meaning of your chosen theme. There is still no guarantee that anyone else will be satisfied. Nor need they be. The important thing is that each one feels for himself the specific expressive quality of a theme or, similarly, an entire piece of music. And if it is a great work of art, don't expect it to mean exactly the same thing to you each time you return to it.

The third plane on which music exists is the sheerly musical plane. Besides the pleasurable sound of music and the expressive feeling that it gives off, music does exist in terms of the notes themselves and of their manipulation. Most listeners are not sufficiently conscious of this third plane. It is very important for all of us to become more alive to music on its sheerly musical plane. After all, an actual musical material is being used. The intelligent listener must be prepared to increase his awareness of the musical material and what happens to it. He must hear the melodies, the rhythms, the harmonies, the tone colors in a more conscious fashion. But above all he must, in order to follow the line of the composer's thought, know something of the principles of musical form. Listening to all of these elements is listening on the sheerly musical plane.

Let me repeat that I have split up mechanically the three separate planes on which we listen merely for the sake of greater clarity. Actually, we never listen on one or the other of these planes. What we do is to correlate them—listening in all three ways at the same time. It takes no mental effort, for we do it instinctively.

(Copland, 2011, pp.7-13)

Step 2 We can take two Chinese and Western paintings as examples to illustrate and interpret the two perspectives in appreciating and understanding art works. We propose the pair of Chinese and Dutch landscape paintings from about the same time in history, i.e., *View of Delft* (Figure 7.21) by the Dutch artist Johannes Vermeer (1632–1675) and *Landscapes of the Four Seasons* (Figure 7.22) by Shi Tao (石涛, 1642–1707) in Qing Dynasty. You can also compare another two paintings by Chinese and Western artist from approximately the same time. Think about this question: According to Copland and Dutton, what do people look for in a painting? What can people get from the two paintings in each of the planes or relevant items?

Step 3 Organize a small seminar to present and discuss in a group your ideas about appreciating Chinese and Western paintings. Each of the speakers should write a short essay (750–1,000 words, including references) or prepare a (video) presentation (7–10 minutes) on the topic

"What to look for in a painting".

Figure 7.21
View of Delft by Johannes Vermeer

Figure 7.22
Landscapes of the Four Seasons by Shi Tao

Activity 7-5 In Section 7.3 we quote the "onion" model of culture levels (Figure 7.20) by Hofstede et al. (2010) to illustrate how convenient it is to promote cultural "symbols" in cross-cultural communication.

In recent decades, the development of cultural products has become a trend in promoting artworks and cultures worldwide. For example, Rijksmuseum, or the Dutch National Museum in Amsterdam, the Netherlands, offers a biennial art and design prize Rijksstudio Award and invites everyone to create their own masterpiece inspired by the Rijksmuseum's collection (high-resolution images available for free download via its web platform). The Palace Museum in Beijing also develops various creative products from their collection of artworks.

How are cultural products designed?

Lin et al. (2007) proposed a Cultural Product Design Model (Figure 7.23) which consists of three main parts: conceptual model, research methods, and design process. As they explained:

Figure 7.23
Cultural product design model

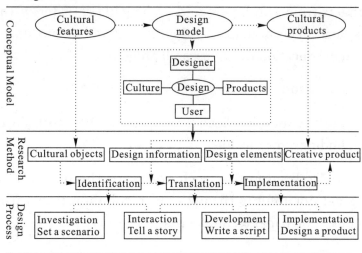

(Adapted from Lin et al. 2007, p.149)

> The conceptual model focuses on how to extract cultural features from cultural objects and then transfer these features to a design model to design cultural products. The research method consists of three steps: identification, translation and implementation, to extract cultural features from original cultural objects (identification), transfer them to design information and design elements (translation), and finally design a cultural product (implementation).
>
> Based on the cultural product design model, the cultural product was designed using scenario and story-telling approaches. In

a practical design process, four steps are used to design a cultural product, namely, investigation (set a scenario), interaction (tell a story), development (write a script), and implementation (design a product).

(Lin et al., 2007, pp.148–149).

Step 1 Read the following project introduction and use the cultural product design model to design a brochure for an outreach program for international students including the theme, introduction, duration, venue and plan of the event.

The International Dunhuang Project (IDP): The Silk Road Online

IDP is a ground-breaking international collaboration to make information and images of all manuscripts, paintings, textiles and artifacts from Dunhuang and archaeological sites of the Eastern Silk Road freely available on the Internet and to encourage their use through educational and research programs.

Conservation

Conservation has been a core part of IDP's work since the start. Its founding aims include:

— To develop new techniques for the preservation of the original documents through close collaboration with research chemists and paper technologists.

— To promote common standards of preservation methods and documentation.

— To store the artifacts in the best possible environment and reduce handling to a minimum.

IDP works with conservators and conservation scientists from institutions worldwide to achieve these aims. It organizes regular conservation conferences and conservation panels at other conferences. These are to enable conservators and scientists to meet, discuss their recent work and find out about new techniques. IDP also publishes books and papers as well as taking an active role in conservation research with conservators and scientists worldwide.

> *Education & Outreach*
>
> IDP aims to bring these wonderful resources to the attention of people outside the scholarly world by talks, publications, educational events and exhibitions. IDP staff regularly give lectures to a wide variety of audiences worldwide, both at academic conferences and in more informal and public settings, including schools, bookshops and local societies. Apart from writing and editing the IDP Newsletter, published twice a year (available on request), IDP staff regularly contribute articles to various journals and magazines. These include reports on IDP, general articles at all levels on conservation, Buddhism, Silk Road history and other topics related to the manuscript finds, as well as the results of their research based on the manuscripts themselves. The web site carries educational sites and projects on My IDP. These are authored by individual IDP staff and are intended to be accessible to a wide audience, from school-children and students to travelers and others. Over the next few years, IDP is developing a greatly enhanced education and outreach program to bring these unique resources to schoolchildren and scholars worldwide. It will be building collaborations with universities and projects involved in education worldwide. Details are given on the education pages.
>
> (Source: http://idp.bl.uk/about)

Step 2 Reflect critically on your process of creating the brochure and keep notes on your reflections about, for example,

- how you pick up the cultural features and decide on the theme,
- what elements from the culture features are used or highlighted in the brochure,
- what is your research method in designing elements for the creative, and
- what scenario and factors you have considered when preparing for telling the story, etc.

7.5 Chapter Summary

A large part of this chapter reviews the development and divergence of visual arts in China and the West. Along the development of the cultures, visual art became more and more vivid and lifelike in the West, and more and more expressive and individualized in China. Later, after the Renaissance in Europe and introduction of Western cultures in China, artists began to notice other alternative perspectives. What we should be aware of, in the process of reviewing Chinese and Western visual arts, is the interactions between art and culture, or between cultural practices and values. In reviewing the major styles in art history, we should keep in mind the mainstreams of cultural influence, the reflection of their time in those works, and the unity within historical style periods (Fleming, 1980, pp.15–17).

It should also be noted that in 7.1 and 7.2 we give some most visible examples from mainly the *High culture* (see Section 1.3.2) because they are the representative parts of symbols that remain traceable in our historical heritage. We are aware of the fact that a tremendous amount of folk artifacts were submerged in the sea of history both in China and the Western countries. Along with the development of mainstream cultures, the folk art has been distilled, developed and inherited by generations of ordinary people. Modern aesthetics is no longer limited to only works of "Heroes" like those classical paintings and sculptures in the museums, but developed on the basis of all art forms. Dutton's (2009) list of core items of art in Section 7.3, for example, can be applied to all art forms, and Lin et al. (2007) proposed the cultural product design model (Figure 7.23) for promoting the aboriginal culture in Taiwan, China. The easy access to the Internet and AI enables people from various places of the world to appreciate, share, study and create artworks online. Cross-cultural communications in visual arts happen every minute in the world. It is our hope that by the models we provide in 7.3 and 7.4, we could realize more the value of artifacts from different cultures, and make it possible for all people in the world to share the beauty of Chinese visual arts.

7.6 Case Study Assignment

Please read the article below and answer the following questions.

Works by Chinese Artist Celebrate Van Gogh's Genius

By Yuan Shenggao

An ardent admirer of Vincent van Gogh, contemporary Chinese artist Zeng Fanzhi created a series of vibrant new paintings for a special exhibition at the Van Gogh Museum in Amsterdam.

The select presentation started on Oct. 20 and lasts until Feb. 25, 2018.

It displays five works, either inspired by Van Gogh's famous paintings or using a similar theme, to pay tribute to the legendary Dutch artist in a special way.

Three portraits of Van Gogh, selected from six that Zeng painted from Van Gogh's original self-portraits, are spotlighted in the exhibition.

Van Gogh's style, appearance and personality are united in his many self-portraits, and Zeng replicated the Dutch artist's works before covering them with his own, distinctive, swirling lines.

According to Zeng, 54, by paying homage to the original pieces, he wanted to experience the way Van Gogh looked at himself, and the creative exercise made him familiar with the thought processes of the great post-impressionist master.

Zeng then added layers of his signature lines, until the image was again covered up, as if placing his identity over that of Van Gogh, before he finally rebuilt the image to conclude the "visual dialogue".

Self-portraits are an extremely personal form of creative expression for Zeng, who has explored his own likeness through them during different stages of his career.

"It's a process of observing and understanding myself better," Zeng said.

Besides Zeng's homage portraits, a painting inspired by Van Gogh's famous piece *Wheatfield with Crows* is showcased next to the original, as both artists have sought inspiration in landscapes.

The last piece, called *Boots*, was created by Zeng in 2009 and is put next to Van Gogh's still-life painting *Shoes*.

In Zeng's works, which come alive with their sinuous lines, the modern artist links his own style and identity to the life and work of Van Gogh.

"Before now, my understanding of Van Gogh was as 'a great artist'," Zeng said before the launch of the exhibition.

"But through the creation of these works, I found that I gradually had a deeper understanding of him—not the literal kind, but experiencing, as an artist, some momentary emotions of another artist."

A native of Wuhan in Hubei Province who moved to Beijing in the early 1990s, Zeng has stood out as one of the most successful contemporary Chinese artists in recent years.

Zeng's art responds to his immersion in a more superficial environment, and his influential *Mask* series portrays the tensions between the artist's dominant existential concerns and an ironic treatment of the pomposity and posturing inherent in his contemporary urban life.

Over the years, he has held solo exhibitions not only in China but worldwide, in cities including Barcelona, Paris, London and New York.

"What I paint is, of course, my life, so Chinese people can understand my works better."

"But I don't want to remain a very regional artist—an artist in Wuhan or in Beijing, but be part of the world's art," said Zeng during the fourth Award of Art China event in 2010.

The presentation of Zeng's latest work at the Van Gogh Museum is the first in a world tour.

(Source: http://www.chinadaily.com.cn)

Questions:

(1) When re-creating the paintings of Van Gogh, Zeng Fanzhi found that he "gradually had a deeper understanding of him (Van Gogh)". What elements in visual art (e.g., in Dutton's (2009) list of core items) made it possible for him to have "a deeper understanding" across cultures? How?

(2) Zeng didn't want to "remain a very regional artist" and he wanted to be a world artist. Is it easy for Chinese arts to be appreciated by Western people? Reviewing the Chinese painting examples in this chapter, or pick up any other one of your favorites, by using the cultural product design model in 7.4, can you design a product or some products inspired by the painting? Can you draft a promotion/marketing plan of your product for

an International Art Fair?

(3) If you can promote artworks, you can promote artists, too. Search online for the websites of the local artists in your city or town and find one with the potential to be promoted overseas but the English web page looks not quite ready yet. Contact the artists and see if you can meet and discuss how you can help to design a better English web page, based on what you know about aesthetics and cross-cultural communication. Yes, you would be well advised to do some homework before you go. List out all your advice and support them with evidence from literature and facts.

References

Copland, A. (2011). *What to listen for in music.* Signet.

Dutton, D. (2009). *The art instinct: Beauty, pleasure, and human evolution.* Bloomsbury Press.

Eno, R. (2015). *Traditional Chinese painting—The literati tradition (course reading).* http://www.indiana.edu/~ealc100/Art1.html

Fleming, W. (1994). *Art & ideas (9th edition).* Cambridge: Wadsworth Publishing

Geng, R. (2021). Study on Giuseppe Castiglione, a court painter in the Qing Dynasty. *Open Journal of Social Sciences, 9,* 193-203. http://doi: 10.4236/jss.2021.99014

Gombrich, E. H. & Gombrich, L. (2023). *The story of art.* Phaidon Press.

Hofstede, G., Hofstede, G. J., & Minkov, M. (2010). *Cultures and organizations: Software of the mind* (3rd edition.). McGraw-Hill.

Holliday, A. (2011). *Intercultural communication and ideology.* Sage.

Kant, I. (1914). *Kant's critique of judgment.* https://oll.libertyfund.org/titles/1217

Lin, R. , Sun, M. X. , Chang, Y. P. , Chan, Y. C. , & Huang, Y. C. Springer. (2007). *Designing "culture" into modern product: A case study of cultural product design.* Springer.

Ruskin J. (1903). Modern painters. In Cook E. T., & Wedderburn A. (Eds.), The complete works of John Ruskin. Longmans.

Schein, E. (1984). Coming to a new awareness of organizational culture. *Sloan Management Review, 25*(2): 3-16.

Yang, H. (2017). Discussion about the influence of Western painting teaching on the fine arts in the Qing Dynasty. In: *Proceedings of the 2016 3rd International Conference* on *Education, Language, Art and Inter-cultural Communication* (ICELAIC 2016). [online] 2016 3rd International Conference on Education, Language, Art and Inter-cultural Communication (ICELAIC 2016). Atlantis Press. https://doi.org/10.2991/icelaic-16.2017.146.

Yang, X., Barnhart, R. M., Nie, C. Z., Cahill, J., Lang, S. J., & Hung, W. (2002). *Three thousand years of Chinese paintings.* Yale University Press.

Pan, T. S. (2019). *Zhongguo huihua shi [Histroy of Chinese Painting].* The Commercial Press.

Shi, Y. G., & Zhang, F. (2011). *Shoubai: jiawunian de zhongri juezhan [First defeat: the Sino-Janpanese decisive battle in 1894].* Phoenix Publishing & Media Group.

Zou, Y. G. (2009). *Xiaoshan huapu [Picture spectrum by Xiaoshan].* Shandong Pictorial Publishing House.

Dutch art historian, Joyce M.M. van der Smit-Meijer, kindly offered us suggestions when revising the first version of the Chapter.

Comparing Cultures Through Poetry

CHEN Dadi, GE Dongmei

8.1 Concrete Experience

Activity 8-1 Read the story and answer the following questions.

> **"Everlasting Classics": U.S. PhD Remixes Hit Song with Ancient Chinese**
>
> *Jiang Qingrui*
>
> American Christine Welch sang a new version of the Chinese pop song "A Million Possibilities," with lyrics inspired by works of Chinese ancient philosopher Zhuangzi, on the latest edition of "Everlasting Classics," a variety show on China Central Television (CCTV).
>
> The song was renamed "The Butterfly Dream: A Million Possibilities." "The Butterfly Dream" is one of the most well-known stories in the ancient Daoist classic *Zhuangzi*, a book that gathered the philosophical theory of Zhuangzi and the descendants of the same school.
>
> The adapted version used more symbols relating to Zhuangzi, including butterflies, dreams, Penglai fairyland, etc. It also kept the original terms like "tears of the clouds," "snowflakes" and "winter night," reflecting a Chinese classical beauty.

All of the symbols create a graceful, restrained and poetic setting to the song. When the words flowed out in her clear and steady voice, she stirred empathy from the crowd of listeners.

In one part, the rhythm sped up, creating a rap-like modern feeling to the ancient classic-based song.

The lyrics are a combination of original lines from literature by Zhuangzi, a thinker in the Warring States Period (475-221 BCE), and Li Bai, a famous poet in the Tang Dynasty (618-907). Welch also used some lines of her own, making it a mash-up of old and new.

She has a bachelor's degree in Asian and Middle Eastern Language and Civilization from North Western University. Now she is in a PhD program for Chinese Literature and Culture at the University of Wisconsin-Madison.

This is not her first literary creation in Chinese. Previously, she managed to publish a poetry collection called *Christine's Book,* which includes her original lyrics and poems in both English and Chinese. Some of the works are even done in ancient Chinese.

The pop song she adapted, "A Million Possibilities", was created by composer Skot Suyama and produced in 2014. Welch is also the lyricist and original singer of this Chinese-language piece. The song soon gained great popularity in China after its release and remains a hit.

Kang Zhen, a Chinese literature professor and guest on the show, said, "The thinking pattern (she used), is not only a Chinese way of thinking, but she sees the world through Chinese ancient philosophy and poetry art."

"I believe the number of young people like her is not merely one or two," he said, "but a lot. All the thinking young people across the world will realize, inside the Chinese ancient philosophy and poetry, there is wisdom, poetic beauty and a driving force that can invigorate their desire for life."

(Source: https://news.cgtn.com/news/)

Questions:

(1) Have you heard the song "A Million Possibilities"? How do you like it? Compared with other Chinese pop songs, is there anything special about

Christine Welch's lyrics?

(2) Welch made an adapted version, i.e., "The Butterfly Dream: A Million Possibilities", for the show. Compared with the original version, which one do you prefer? Why?

(3) Do you agree with what Prof. Kang Zhen said, i.e., Welch sees the world through Chinese ancient philosophy and poetry art? If yes, can you find any evidence to support it in her lyrics? If not, in your opinion, what is the Chinese way of thinking, or the perspective of Chinese ancient philosophy and poetry, about time and love?

8.2 Reflective Observation

Art is *"visible but often not decipherable"* (Schein, 1984, p4. see also Section 1.3.1). Poetry can be a typical example, especially in high-context cultures like the Chinese culture. Similar to the way we appreciate literati paintings, we need a lot of information beyond the language itself to understand what a Chinese poem means. In a way, comparing cultures through poetry is like comparing the coding systems of different cultures, which includes not only the poetic traditions, but also philosophies of beauty or aesthetics, social conventions, and cultural norms.

Activity 8-2   Please read the two poems, and discuss the following questions.

Renouncement

By Alice Meynell

I must not think of thee[1]; and, tired yet strong,
I shun the thought that lurks in all delight —
The thought of thee—and in the blue heaven's height,
And in the dearest passage of a song.

Oh, just beyond the fairest thoughts that throng
This breast the thought of thee waits, hidden yet bright
But it must never, never come in sight;

---

1. In Old and Middle English, people used different words to mean "you". "Thou" is equivalent to modern "you" as the singular subject (主语). "Thee" means you as the singular object (宾语). Similarly, they also used "thy" (modern equivalent "your") and "thine" (modern equivalent "yours").

I must stop short of thee the whole day long.¹

But when sleep comes to close each difficult day,
When night gives pause to the long watch I keep,
And all my bonds I needs must loose apart,
Must doff my will as raiment laid away,²
With the first dream that comes with the first sleep
I run, I run, I am gathered to thy heart.

蝶恋花

[宋]晏殊

槛菊愁烟兰泣露，
罗幕轻寒，
燕子双飞去。
明月不谙离恨苦，
斜光到晓穿朱户。

昨夜西风凋碧树，
独上高楼，
望尽天涯路。
欲寄彩笺兼尺素³,
山长水阔知何处。

Questions:

(1) What are the objects/things mentioned in the poems? Are they similar or different? Can you give some examples?

(2) What do the two poets want to tell us?

(3) Do you know anything about the two poets and the popular idea about love in the time of the poets? You can do a small desk research and share your findings with your friends.

(4) Can you explain the differences by relating to their respective cultural backgrounds?

---

1. I must stop missing you for the whole day. There is an interesting contrast between "short" and "long" in this line.

2. The word "doff" in the past means to remove an item of clothing, especially, a hat. Raiment: clothing. The two lines seem to describe taking off clothing before bed. But the poetess also compared her thought to bonds, and her will to raiment, which need to be "loose apart" and "laid away".

3. 彩笺，指诗人写此诗用的诗笺；尺素，指书信。这句的意思是，我想用这首诗兼作书信寄给你。

(5) How do you understand the use or benefit of poetry (or literature) in our life and culture?

(6) How do you understand the relationship between poetry and culture?

8.2.1 Sonnet and *Ci* (词): A comparison

> A rose by any other name would smell as sweet.
>
> — William Shakespeare (1564—1616), *Romeo and Juliet*

Love is the commonest theme of poetry. For people in different cultures, love might be expressed in different ways in poetry. The two poems quoted above, i.e., "Renouncement" by Alice Meynell, and "Die Lian Hua" by Yan Shu (晏殊) showed us how love was described in the classic poetry of two cultures.

We might have noticed that love was expressed differently in the two poems. Meynell spoke like an obsessed lady, starting with a "renouncement" of the thought of her lover, because the thought was "tired yet strong." She was struggling with this renouncement. How strange that a poem begins with "I don't want to think about you anymore!" If we read on, we will soon find out that such renouncement was not because of any miserable or unpleasant experience. Instead, the thought of her lover existed strongly "in all delight." She declined from the thought only because she was tortured by the thought of her lover when she could not see him. However, when she finally ended the day of thought, it was time for sleep. She "ran" to the heart of her lover, and they could reunite in the dream. The poem starts in an uncommon way and ends in surprise, with every line connected to the obsession and inner struggle.

The Chinese *Ci* by Yan Shu is quite different. It describes the painful attachment to a faraway lover in the tone of a lady's voice. The poem starts with a gloomy and depressive atmosphere by describing the house and objects with the words suggesting coldness, loneliness and sadness. Why did the poet not start the poem about human love simply with humans, but things? And besides, things do not suggest happiness or sadness. It is only the feelings of human beings that change their views. In other words, we can imagine that in the eyes of the abandoned lover, everything is sad. The misery and sorrow was enhanced in the second stanza of the poem, when the lady wished to send the poem as a letter to her lover but did not know where he was.

If the English sonnet suggests sweet joy of thought and a sweet dream of reunion, the Chinese *Ci* is filled with complete despair and desperation. These two poems can be taken as good examples to show two distinctive styles of English sonnets and Chinese *Ci*. The former starts with surprising remarks of a person, the latter with sentimental descriptions of the environment. The former reveals the inner conflict, obsession, and sentimentality in love, and the latter with disappointment and complaint. The former depicts a sentimental lover, while the latter a disappointed one. The sentimentality and passion in the former may finally lead to disillusions and philosophical meditations, while the complaint and despair in the latter may lead to self-pity on the misfortunes in life. We can further explore the causes of such difference when we review the development of the two styles in history.

Activity 8-3 When reading further the two poems by Alice Meynell and Yan Shu (see Activity 8-2), we find one of the differences between them was the beginning. The Chinese *Ci* begins with things, instead of people, even though the two poems are both about human love. Let us do a little but bold test. Please rewrite the first four lines of the English sonnet by whatever things you think can convey the poet's ideas, avoiding saying "I" or any other words suggesting human beings. You can also rewrite the first five lines of the Chinese *Ci*, but begin with 我, or any words indicating a person. You don't need to change the language when you rewrite, or seriously take it as writing a poem. You can compare with your classmates about your draft, and discuss your new versions of poems. What have you gained, or missed?

To follow closely the interactions in history between poetry and culture, we take two of the classic poetic styles as an example, i.e., English sonnets and Chinese *Ci* (We also interchange the term *Ci* with lyrics or Chinese lyrics sometimes.). The popularity of sonnet and *Ci* seemed to be a fashion in their times. The poets at that time exerted all their passion in writing in the styles and established their own reputations by creative and individualized works. The popularity of the styles was also accompanied by the popular trend of thought. Through the review and comparison of the two styles, we probably will understand how poetry becomes a voice of culture, and see what cultural difference we can see from reading poems.

8.2.2 The development of sonnet

Sonnet is a lyric poem of 14 lines, usually in iambic pentameters with considerable variations in rhyme patterns (Cuddon, 1977, pp.628–629). The style originated from the Italian *canzone* (Italian for "song") of the 13th century. The early Italian sonnet, also named after the famous poet as Petrarchan sonnet, consisted of an 8-line section followed by a 6-line section. When it was introduced to England, the English style (named after the famous Shakespeare) can be divided into three 4-line sections and a pair of lines in the end, resulting anyway in 14 lines altogether. The style was also characterized by a turn in idea occurring in the middle for the two-section structure or the second or third division in the four-section structure (see Figure 8.1 which shows also the typical rhyming patterns of each kind).

Sonnet was introduced to other European countries in the 16th century together with the popular trend of Renaissance, followed by an outburst of many sonneteers. "*No major poet—... no minor one either—in Italian, German, French, Spanish, and English has failed to write sonnets*" (Walter Mönch, as cited in Oppenheimer, 1982, p.290). Why was sonnet so popular in Europe at that time? If we had read hymns and songs only from the priests for five hundred years, perhaps we would also be thrilled to something that is different, human and romantic. The poetic style is short and not difficult to imitate, convenient for any argument and resolution of a topic (e.g., if one loves the person, why, and what he or she will do), and can always be connected to the Italian fashion of renewing the ancient Greek and Roman culture. It is a symbol of Renaissance in literature.

Figure 8.1

Structures of Petrarchan and Shakespearean sonnets

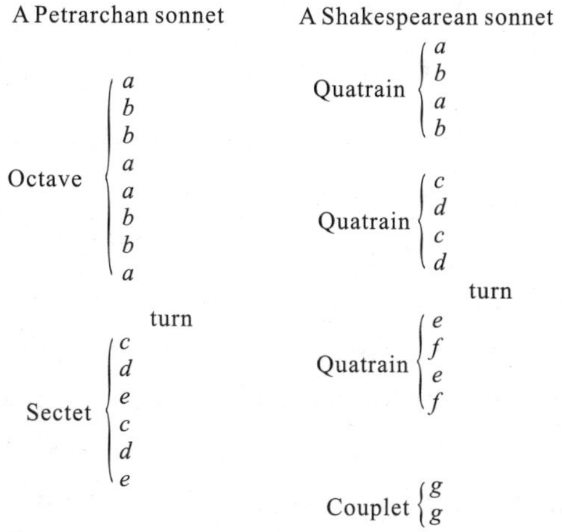

	A Petrarchan sonnet	A Shakespearean sonnet
Octave	a, b, b, a, a, b, b, a	Quatrain: a, b, a, b
		Quatrain: c, d, c, d
	turn	turn
Sectet	c, d, e, c, d, e	Quatrain: e, f, e, f
		Couplet: g, g

The poets of the Renaissance, similar to the writers and artists at that time, were inspired by the findings of the classical ancient Greco-Roman literature. They wrote poems and poetic dramas based on the stories at that time, but with new meaning. They alluded to the romantic or tragic heroes or stories in Greek and Roman mythology, comparing people in the real world to those heroes. Benefited from the spread of printing in the latter part of the 15th century, humanist philosophy and literature soon spread over Europe. Platonic ideas were revived and put to the service of Christianity. The search for pleasures of the senses and a critical and rational spirit completed the ideological panorama of the time. Humans, once again, became the center of the world. As Shakespeare said via the hero of his famous play, *Hamlet*:

> What a piece of work is a man, how noble in reason, how infinite in faculties, in form and moving, how express and admirable in action, how like an angel in apprehension, how like a god!

(*Hamlet*, Act Ⅱ, Scene 2)

The poetic style of sonnet was popular along with the fashion of translating the love poems by the Italian poets such as Petrarch and Dante, whose works were admired by people all over Europe. After sonnet was introduced to England, the poets tried every means to make it more harmonious to the English accent. For example, Surrey changed the original rhyme scheme by adding more rhymes. He adapted the rhyme scheme of sonnet to the fact that there are fewer vowel-ending words as rhyming words in English than in Italian. His new model of *abab cdcd efef gg* came to be known later as the *Shakespearean sonnet*, because Shakespeare wrote with the model a sonnet sequence that was so popular and became a classic in English poetry. After several decades of adaptation from Italian to English through translation and imitation, sonnet was finally established in England as one of the most popular metrical poetic forms. Figure 8.2[1] shows how sonnet developed and changed after it was introduced to England.

The English sonnet style was named after Shakespeare for at least two fair reasons. Not only because he showed a master hand in his sonnets, but also he gave the imported style new contemporary English blood. Like some of his plays, Shakespeare (Figure 8.3) wrote sonnets for the people in his time, instead of heroes in legends or stories in the Bible. In Shakespeare's *Sonnets*, the beautiful character being addressed is most often a young man, rather than an idealized female as in former sonnets. Shakespeare adds to and varies the Italian sonnets in other ways as well, such as introducing themes of death and aging and the undying fame poetry lends to the self and the beloved. He also makes both the young man and the Dark Lady of the later sonnets less

---

1. Adapted from the concept map in http://cmapspublic.ihmc.us/rid=1159722745555_2058052637_10253/Sonnet.cmap.

than perfect, which is very different from the conventional picture of an ideal beloved saint. Here is one of the most widely known sonnets by Shakespeare.

Figure 8.2
Development of sonnet rhyming schemes in England

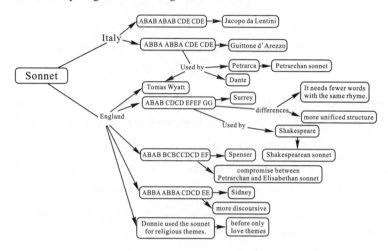

Figure 8.3
The portrait of Shakespeare

William Shakespeare was an English poet and playwright, widely regarded as the greatest writer in the English language and the world's pre-eminent dramatist.

Sonnet 18

By William Shakespeare

Shall I compare thee to a summer's day?
Thou art more lovely and more temperate:
Rough winds do shake the darling buds of May,
And summer's lease hath all too short a date:
Sometime too hot the eye of heaven shines,
And often is his gold complexion dimmed,

> And every fair from fair sometime declines,
> By chance, or nature's changing course untrimmed:
> But thy eternal summer shall not fade,
> Nor lose possession of that fair thou ow'st,
> Nor shall death brag thou wand'rest in his shade,
> When in eternal lines to time thou grow'st:
>   So long as men can breathe or eyes can see,
>   So long lives this, and this gives life to thee.

The poem is a typical Shakespearean sonnet, with 14 lines in three quatrains and a couplet, and iambic pentameter in almost every line. It was considered to be addressed to one of his young and handsome noble friends. The poet praised his charm and beauty with comparison to beautiful things in nature. The theme, however, is that the charm and beauty of his friend will last forever by the power of the poem, which echoes the popular theme at that time that life is short, but art is eternal.

The poem was collected in *Shakespeare's Sonnets*, first published in 1609, with other 153 sonnets (Figure 8.4). The first 126 were considered to be dedicated to a gentleman addressed as Mr. W. H. at the cover page, and the rest 28 to a Dark Lady. The sonnets were written in a semi-autobiographical way in that the readers can follow the sequence of poems to share the poet's joy and sorrow. The poems cherish beauty and love, and inspire readers to imagine the happy time the poet enjoyed with his friend and lover. The sad and distressed poems make them feel sad about his misfortune in life. The collection of the sonnets became popular after its publication and a classic over time.

Figure 8.4
The cover and head pages of *Shakespeare's Sonnets*, published in 1609

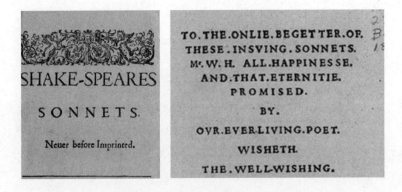

In the 17th century, Rationalism became a mainstream, which regarded reason as the chief source and test of knowledge. Sonnet became old-fashioned, probably due to its connection to emotion and sentimentality. Hardly any lyric poet in that period wrote any sonnet. Poets like Donne and Milton wrote scanty sonnets and often on other themes, such as religion and philosophy. After Milton the sonnet virtually disappeared for over a century. In the 18th century, there were few of excellent sonneteers, except the three forerunners of Romanticism, Thomas Gray, Thomas Warton and William Bowles.

From the end of the 18th century to the mid-19th century, Europe witnessed dramatic changes brought by industrial revolution, and great social turmoil during and after the French revolution. The dissatisfaction against the age-long aristocratic social norms and the confines of this scientific rationalism gave rise to an artistic, literary and intellectual movement called Romanticism. Romantic poets and artists regarded the strong emotion as a true source of aesthetic experience and artistic creation. They embraced nature instead of machines. They sang for the true feelings and free imagination in passionate but simple language. Sonnet was dramatically revived as a classic vehicle of emotions. Wordsworth, Keats, Shelley and Coleridge all wrote splendid sonnets.

The following Victorian period in England was a long period of peace, prosperity, refined sensibilities and national self-confidence for Britain. In Europe and United States had a similar atmosphere.[1] A large number of poets reestablished the sonnet form, and in particular the sonnet-sequence about love. When English politicians and businessmen looked for fortunes overseas, poets and artists looked inside their heart. This is an era of transition between tradition and modern innovations. English Victorian poets such as Dante Gabriel Rossetti, Christina Rossetti, and Elizabeth Barrett Browning (Figure 8.5) were prominent sonneteers to explore the charm of sonnet, with meditation about love, faith, life, and truth.

One of the major works of sonnet in the Victorian period is Elizabeth Barrett Browning's *Sonnets from the Portuguese* (1847–1850). Similar to *Shakespeare's Sonnets*, the poetess also wrote a semi-autobiographical work recording her love to her husband, Robert Browning, who was also a brilliant poet. Robert admired Elizabeth's poems before seeing her. He wrote her a letter to tell her how much he loved her poems. When he finally met her in 1845, one of the most famous courtships in literature began. Six years his elder and an invalid, she could not believe that the vigorous and worldly Browning really loved her as much as he professed to, and her doubts were expressed in these sonnets, together with her

---

1. The latter half of the Victorian age roughly coincided with the first portion of the Belle Époque era of continental Europe and the Gilded Age of the United States.

bliss, gratitude and hope. She wrote these poems over the next two years, till they got married. At her husband's insistence, the second edition of her *Poems* included her love sonnets. Here is one of the sonnets:

Figure 8.5
Elizabeth Barrett Browning (1806–1861)

Sonnet 43

By Elizabeth Barrett Browning

How do I love thee? Let me count the ways.
I love thee to the depth and breadth and height
My soul can reach, when feeling out of sight
For the ends of Being and ideal Grace.
I love thee to the level of every day's
Most quiet need, by sun and candlelight.
I love thee freely, as men strive for Right
I love thee purely, as they turn from Praise.
I love thee with the passion put to use
In my old griefs, and with my childhood's faith.
I love thee with a love I seemed to lose
With my lost saints—I love thee with the breath,
Smiles, tears, of all my life!—and, if God choose,
I shall but love thee better after Death.

The poem is quite different from those in Elizabethan time in both language and structure. The words are more plain than formal. The poem, though in the form of a sonnet with strict rhyme and rhythm scheme, is more like a free verse when the end of a line is void because the sentence needs to be finished till the next line or even later. The bound of meters became flexible and the poets used it more creatively in the 19th Century. But still, metrical poems became old fashioned since they represent more constrains and traditions than freedom and innovation. Since the Edwardian period (1901–1910) when more modernist literary thought became popular, few poets have shown much interest in the sonnet (Cuddon, 1977).

8.2.3 The development of *Ci*

Similar to sonnet, Chinese *Ci* originated from folk songs, but almost a thousand years earlier than the former. It was developed in the 6th century from earlier metrical poems (乐府), and became very popular from the 8th to 11th century. Since the establishment of the imperial musical office (教坊) in the Tang Dynasty, folk songs can be played together with the classic ones in the royal palace. Some poetic styles, such as *Jue Ju* (绝句), a lyric form of four lines, were put in tune with music. Many famous poets, such as Li Bai (李白) and Bai Juyi (白居易), were summoned to the imperial musical office to show their talents to the Emperor and his family. Many of the imperial officials, and even the Emperor himself knew how to compose *Ci*.

Since the turmoil in the year 755, a lot of musicians were driven out of the royal musical office. They were reduced to singers or composers in Musical Inns (or Singing Houses, 伎馆) all over the country. These musical inns also welcomed such the renowned poets as Bai Juyi, Liu Yuxi (刘禹锡), Wen Tingyun (温庭筠), and Wei Zhuang (韦庄), who were inspired by the beautiful singers, and composed right on the spot a lot of poems in tune with their music. Wei Zhuang described in one of his poems, in tune with *Pu Sa Man*, leisure and carnal pleasure when he was young.

菩萨蛮其三

[唐] 韦庄

如今却忆江南乐
当时年少春衫薄
骑马斜倚桥
满楼红袖招
翠屏金屈曲
醉入花丛宿
此度见花枝
白头誓不归

It was popular at that time to compare women to flowers in lyrics. So the first collection of *Ci*, published before the year 971, was also entitled *Huajianji* (《花间集》), or the *Collection of Love Lyrics*. It recorded many of the works by the poets in the Tang Dynasty and later eras.

The musical inns became a popular place for social activities and entertainment in the Song Dynasty. There were inns everywhere in a populated city or town. Like many of the bars today, they had professional singers and musicians. Imagine when we sit with our friends comfortably in one of those inns in a warm spring afternoon, enjoying the nice taste of wine, talking about everything and nothing, watching people in the streets, and what else do we expect? In a modern bar, we often have some background music. In the Song Dynasty, we would not be bored. The songs by the young, beautiful singers can easily relax us with their soothing, siren-like voice. The melody might be familiar to everyone because it has become popular for a while, but every time people hear different lyrics. Some of them are elegant and tasteful, others nostalgic or sentimental. If there was a poet among the guests, and he (or rarely, she) would like to try, he can also fill in the tune with his improvised lyrics, and take the pride to share with his friends through the performance of the singers ... For a moment in life, the audiences forget about the stern faces of the officials, the scholarly doctrines of Confucianism,[1] the cold, fussy bureaucracy, the unfairness in society, and their uncontrollable fate. Just like the literati painters, when writing and sharing lyrics, the poet was free, or let us say, freer to express himself, and his talent as a literary man can earn him applause, admiration, or even love.

雨霖铃

[宋] 柳永

寒蝉凄切, 对长亭晚, 骤雨初歇。
都门帐饮无绪, 留恋处、兰舟催发。
执手相看泪眼, 竟无语凝噎。
念去去、千里烟波, 暮霭沉沉楚天阔。

多情自古伤离别。
更那堪、冷落清秋节。
今宵酒醒何处, 杨柳岸、晓风残月。
此去经年, 应是良辰、好景虚设。
便纵有, 千种风情, 更与何人说。

---

1. The popularity of love lyrics was explained by modern scholars as a reaction against traditional repression of human instinct of pursuing love and happiness, and an early awareness of humanity (Xie, 1999).

That might be the reason why the poets in the Song Dynasty (960–1279) became so fascinated by *Ci*. Even the emperors, like Song Taizong and Song Renzong, enjoyed making new tunes and lyrics. Many new tunes were created, from Short Lyric (no more than 58 or 62 characters, 小令) to various kinds of Slow Lyric (between 70 and 240 characters, 慢词). People wrote and sang different lyrics at various occasions, from festivals, household celebrations, to gatherings of family or friends. They can also hear people singing lyrics everywhere like popular songs today. It was said that the works of Liu Yong (柳永), one of the most popular poets at that time, can be heard wherever there was a well for drinking[1].

Liu Yong was one of the most talented poets in composing love lyrics. He had no interest in politics, and lived a carefree life by writing poems and entertaining himself in musical inns. The poem *Yu Lin Ling* described his sorrow when he recalled his departure from his lover.

As shown in the example, a lot of the poems in that period described people's sadness, loneliness, and depression. Why were the poets so unhappy? Is love or life so hard for them? They might be, but another way to read these sad poems is to take them as complaints against their own misfortune. Like abandoned women, some of poets felt ignored by the Emperors, who were the only hope to them to achieve their ambition of benefiting people with their talents. Now they languished over their misfortunes in political life, waiting for the time when they could be noticed and promoted no matter how bleak the hope was, just like an abandoned wife who has no idea when her husband will return.

The poem *Die Lian Hua* by Su Shi (Figure 8.6) might be one of such kinds. It was not expressed in the voice of a miserable lover. Actually, we do not know who was speaking. The poem is quite implicit, like a traveler talking to himself when passing someone's door. We can read it as a cute, lovely, and sarcastic poem about the scene the poet saw in the spring. But it was said the poet asked one of his concubines to sing the poem on the trip when he was demoted and dismissed from the royal court. Why did he think of this poem in exile? Did the poet try to comfort and mock himself in the poem to relieve his despair at that moment?

In the Southern Song Dynasty, when Confucian school of idealist philosophy advocated by Cheng Yi (程颐) in the mid-Northern Song Dynasty, steadily gaining its influence, *Ci* was considered as "useless nonsense" which

---

1. 凡有井水饮处，即能歌柳词。

"*betrays the truth, loses justice, and harms reason.*"[1] Philosophers thought the personal desire of comfort, which most lyrics were about, should be abandoned to highlight the universal truth.[2] This thought was rejected by many scholars and poets, but since the social parameters changed, their attitude towards *Ci* also changed.

Figure 8.6
Portrait of Su Shi (1037–1101)

Su Shi, also known as Dong Po, was a Chinese writer, poet, painter, calligrapher, pharmacologist, gastronome, and a statesman of the Song Dynasty.

蝶恋花·春景

[宋] 苏轼

花褪残红青杏小。
燕子飞时，绿水人家绕。
枝上柳绵吹又少。
天涯何处无芳草。

墙里秋千墙外道。
墙外行人，墙里佳人笑。
笑渐不闻声渐悄。
多情却被无情恼

Wars broke out frequently between the minority kingdoms and Song. Millions of people were driven out of their homes, and even

---

1. "无用之赘言" "离真失正，反害于道" (*The Collected Works of Cheng in Henan*, quoted in Xie, 1999:26).
2 灭私欲而天理明 (quoted from Xie, 1959).

the emperor moved his capital from the North to the South. Many poets started to write about their patriotism, their family losses, their memory about the past glory and entertainment with the singers, which vastly echoed in the musical inns (Xie, 1999; Yuan, 2014). An example can be the famous *Man Jiang Hong*, written by general Yue Fei (岳飞), who was regarded as a hero in fighting against the invaders from the North (Figure 8.7).

Figure 8.7
Huan Wo He Shan by Yue Fei (1103–1142)

It means "return my mountains and rivers", or "let's restore our lost land".

满江红·写怀

[宋] 岳飞

怒发冲冠,凭栏处、潇潇雨歇。
抬望眼,仰天长啸,壮怀激烈。
三十功名尘与土,八千里路云和月。
莫等闲、白了少年头,空悲切。

靖康耻,犹未雪。
臣子恨,何时灭。
驾长车踏破,贺兰山缺。
壮志饥餐胡虏肉,笑谈渴饮匈奴血。
待从头、收拾旧山河,朝天阙。

Later works of *Ci* cannot be comparable to those of Song. *The Collected Works of Song Ci* has published nearly 20,000 pieces, many of which became classics for later generations.[1] After China was reunited, the sentimental regrets about the past was no longer a fashion, and *Ci* gave way to *Qu* (曲), or a type of verse in singing, usually based on historical stories. With the extension of various themes other than love, it became unsuitable to be sung. In the Ming Dynasty when Confucian school of idealist philosophy became

---

1. For example, *Ci* were idealized in the Yuan Dynasty as a nobler literary style called *Da Yue* (大乐), or classic music (Shi, 2004). In the later eras, people labeled their styles by the declaration of imitating one of those poets in the Song Dynasty (Hu, 2003; Sun, 2004; Xia & Zhang, 2018; Yuan, 2014).

dominant, few poets wrote *Ci*. People who can sing the lyrics became less and less, and more and more people preferred reading them rather than singing them. In the Qing Dynasty *Ci* was revitalized, but became more delicate with refined words and many historical or literary allusions. Only some of the literary men knew how to compose it. Though *Ci* is no longer popular, the metrical schemes of the tunes remain stable and rarely change through the ages. This consistency maintains *Ci* to be an oral style for music, and may contrast itself with the style of sonnet.

8.2.4 Cross-cultural perspective and modern poetry

Though some people still read and write poems today, the fashion of metrical poetry is gone. Old rules have long been abandoned since the end of the 19th century. Poetry today is more and more commercialized and appears in our life with advertisements more often than for entertainment. Lyrics became a new form of poetry, but with pop songs. In the modern globalized world, people like to try different styles and various perspectives. Instead of sticking to one fashionable and dominant poetic style, we have more and more individualized styles that can hardly be labeled as Eastern or Western.

In the May Fourth movement nearly a hundred years ago, modern Chinese were encouraged to replace the classical language in literature. Poems in Western languages were translated into modern Chinese, and inspired poets to look for new poetic forms for modern Chinese from Western literature. Many literary men, such as Wen Yiduo（闻一多）, Feng Zhi（冯至）, Bian Zhilin（卞之琳）, Tu An（屠岸）, etc., started to write sonnets. Here is one of the sonnets written by Feng Zhi (Figure 8.8).

Figure 8.8
Feng Zhi (1905–1993)

十四行诗 (1)

冯至

我们准备着深深地领受
那些意想不到的奇迹,
在漫长的岁月里忽然有
彗星的出现,狂风乍起;
我们的生命在这一瞬间,
仿佛在第一次的拥抱里
过去的悲欢忽然在眼前
凝结成屹然不动的形体。
我们赞颂那些小昆虫,
它们经过了一次交媾
或是抵御了一次危险,
便结束它们美妙的一生。
我们整个的生命在承受
狂风乍起,彗星的出现。

In the meantime, Asian literature was also introduced to the West. Modern poets were fascinated by the expressive style of Chinese and Japanese poems. In the time when classical meters were seen as old-fashioned and constrained to new aesthetic thoughts, Eastern literature became a model for their artistic innovations. Ezra Pound (Figure 8.9), for example, found inspiration in his reading and translation of Japanese and Chinese poems. He wrote a poem imitating the style of Japanese haiku,[1] which is considered as one of the leading poems of the Imagist tradition, though it is a very short one.

Figure 8.9
Ezra Pound (1885–1972)

Ezra Pound was an American expatriate poet and critic of the early modernist movement. His contribution to poetry began with his promotion of Imagism. (Photo by Alvin Langdon Coburn)

---

1. Haiku (俳句诗) is a Japanese poem of seventeen syllables, in three lines of five, seven, and five, traditionally evoking images of the natural world.

In a Station of the Metro

By Ezra Pound

The apparition of these faces in the crowd;
Petals on a wet, black bough.

The poet wrote in the form of a Japanese haiku. Like ancient Chinese or Japanese poetry, he described images rather than reasoning things out. This is just a short description of a scene which the poet saw in a metro station in Paris. What did he want to say? Nothing, but the image and impression at THAT moment. The transient, fluid, and lively moment was presented like a still-life painting. No meters, no quatrains, no regular length of lines, even without a verb. It is different from any poem ever appeared in history. A moment of life, perhaps, is all the poet wanted to write about. "In a poem of this sort," as Pound himself explained, "one is trying to record the precise instant when a thing outward and objective transforms itself, or darts into a thing inward and subjective." Inward and subjective? Doesn't it sound like what a Chinese poet did hundreds of years ago?

爱的礼物

白马

一支古老的意大利情歌
经过彼特拉克大师吟唱
带着乡土和野草的芬芳
悠然登上了诗的雅座
文艺复兴的亚得里亚海波
又使这隽永迷人的绝唱
荡起轻盈美丽的双桨
飞向世界的各个角落
一支歌填上了诸家新词
也填补了一片片心灵的荒芜
一种调融入了百般情思
也融化了千万个心灵的孤独
这温馨甜蜜的十四行诗
是上苍赐予人间的爱的礼物

As freedom, creativity, and globalisation, etc., become the dominant themes of the modern world, metrical poetic styles like sonnet and *Ci*, which represent convention and constraint, were long abandoned. But we shall not forget that modern poetry and lyrics were actually developed from the classical ones, just like modern arts were born from the womb of classical works. The styles ever invented, no matter classic or modern, no matter Eastern or Western, offer us a vast repertoire for our appreciation, performance, creation and entertainment. The sonnet written by a Chinese modern poet Bai Ma for the style of sonnet, perhaps, can be regarded as a classical one by later generations as well.

Activity 8-4 In this chapter, we compare two poetic styles in two cultures. The research dealing with the literature of two or more different linguistic, cultural or national groups is an academic field known as comparative literature. Through the comparison, we may understand more about these literary works, as well as the relevant cultures. Can you find a pair of short stories, essays, songs, or movies, in both Chinese and Western literature to compare their themes, subject matters, structures, languages, etc., and summarize what you have found in the comparison?

8.3 Abstract Conceptualization

8.3.1 What is poetry?

Poetry was defined differently among cultures and even among poets and literary men in the same culture or era. Usually we define poetry as a literary style different from prose. The elements of poetry are many, e.g., theme, voice, imagery,[1] sound, form, word choice and order, figures of speech, symbol, allegory, allusion, myth, etc. Aristotle's *Poetics* (c. 335 BC) is the earliest-surviving work of dramatic theory and the first surviving philosophical work on literary theory. Aristotle offers in it an account of what he calls "poetry" (a term which in Greek literally means "making" and in this context includes drama—comedy, tragedy, and the satyr play—as well as lyric poetry, epic poetry, and the dithyramb). In the following, we explore the features of poetry in its sound, sight, and "soul".

The sound of poetry

Early poems developed from folk songs (such as some of the poems collected in the Chinese *Shi Jing* (《诗经》), or from a need to retell oral epics (such as the Homeric epics, the *Iliad* and the *Odyssey*). Aristotle (c. 384–

---

1. Imagery means the visually descriptive or figurative language in poetry.

322 BCE) regarded the origin of poetry from the human nature of imitation and their sense of harmony and rhythm.

> It is clear that the general origin of poetry was due to two causes, each of them part of human nature ... Imitation, then, being natural to us—as also the sense of harmony and rhythm, the meters being obviously species of rhythms—it was through their original aptitude, and by a series of improvements for the most part gradual on their first efforts, that they created poetry out of their improvisations.
>
> —Aristotle, *Poetics*

Aristotle considered people's natural instinct to rhythm finally led to the birth of poetry. Then what are the "series of improvements" that help them to create poetry? The answer is *regularity*. Recurring sounds may give human beings a feeling of harmony, such as the sound of water flow, or the songs of birds. If Aristotle was right, the first poem may come out from a line or several lines of a folk song that sounded perfectly with repeating sounds. This pattern of repeating sounds allowed people to put different words in it, express various ideas, and stimulated them to create more patterns, later known as *metrical schemes*. No matter how people name these schemes, they all have a bond with rhythm and rhyme.

Rhythm refers to the regulated flow of words and phrases which is determined by the relation of long and short or stressed and unstressed syllables.[1] In a line of a metrical poem, i.e., a poem in a certain metrical pattern, the words were assigned into regular units. For example, when reading the first two lines of Shakespeare's *Sonnet 18*, we find in each line exactly ten syllables repeating a sound combination consisting of two syllables. In each of the combinations, a weak (or unstressed) syllable is followed by a strong (or stressed) one. We marked out the stressed syllables in bold-face letters, and divided the combinations by slashes.

> **Shall I**/com-**pare**/thee to/a **sum**/-mer's day?/
>
> **Thou art**/more **love**/-ly and/more **tem**/-pe-**rate**:/

---

[1]. A syllable is a unit of sound in words. A single Chinese character usually has only one syllable. But lots of English words have more than one syllable, as decided by the vowels. For example, the word "poetry" contains two syllables, poe-try, while the word "poetic" contains three syllables, po-e-tic (That's probably why they have different stresses.).

春	眠	不	觉	晓
平	平	仄	仄	仄
处	处	闻	啼	鸟
仄	仄	平	平	仄
夜	来	风	雨	声
仄	平	平	仄	平
花	落	知	多	少
平	仄	平	平	仄

The name of such a combination is called an *iamb*. The combinations are called *iambic meters* in poetry. A line consisting of five regular combinations is called *pentameter* (meaning "five meters"). So a line like the above is called *iambic pentameter*. In Chinese language, we only have one-syllable characters like *chun, mian, ping,* and we differentiate the characters of the same sound by four tones and/or in the combination with other characters. Chinese poets generally divide the four tones of the Chinese language into two groups, namely, Level Tones (Ping) and Oblique Tones (Ze)[1]. Ping and Ze thus formed various sound patterns for lines in the poems. Here is an example of a metrical scheme called "Five Words Truncated Verse."[2]

With rhyme, poets can also achieve rhythmic regularity in poems. A rhyme is a repetition of similar sounds in two or more words, most often at the end of lines in poems. In the examples given above, we can easily find rhyming words or characters at the end of the lines. For different metrical schemes, the requirements of end-rhymes are different. Poets in old times created various poetic styles, with different combinations of rhythm and rhyme.

The sight of poetry

Poetry can be defined from the rhetorical features such as repetition, verse form and rhyme. People emphasized the aesthetics which distinguish poetry from more objectively-informative, prosaic forms of writing, such as a news report, a business contract, or the instruction manual of a new mobile phone. Poetry is an art, connected to other art forms, such as music and

---

1. In classical Chinese, the 4 tones are "Ping 平" (can be further sub-divided into "Yin Ping 阴平" and "Yang Ping 阳平"), "Shang 上," "Qu 去" and "Ru 入." The "Yin Ping 阴平" and "Yang Ping 阴平" are grouped under the level tones (Ping 平), while the tones of "Shang 上," "Qu 去" and "Ru 入" are "Oblique Tones (Ze 仄)."

2. 五言绝句。

painting.

To Chinese poets in ancient times, poetry was inseparable from music, perhaps because poems were sung, rather than read in many circumstances, such as royal rituals, banquets, or gatherings of family or friends.

> 诗言志，歌永言，声依永，律和声。
>
> ——《尚书尧典》

> 诗为乐心，声为乐体。
>
> ——[南朝·梁]刘勰，《文心雕龙》

Interestingly, poetry can also be related to painting. Simonides of Ceos (c. 556–468 BCE), a poet in ancient Greece, related poetry to the art of painting. He said, "*Painting is silent poetry, and poetry painting that speaks*". This idea reminds us of a well-known comment made by Su Shi (苏轼), a poet in the Song Dynasty, on the works of Wang Wei (王维):

> 味摩诘之诗，诗中有画；观摩诘之画，画中有诗。

Here is one of the poems written by Wang Wei.

> **鹿柴**
>
> [唐]王维
>
> 空山不见人，
> 但闻人语响。
> 返景入深林，
> 复照青苔上。

The poem describes the scene in the serene wood of a mountain, when the quietness is disturbed by only a few human sounds, and the light of sunset shining upon the mosses of rocks. The scene is vivid before our eyes like a picture. It should be noted that Wang Wei was also recorded in history as one of the pioneers of *literati painting* (see Chapter 7 about visual arts). We can see such a connection between his poems and paintings by the ideal secluded life in nature depicted in both the poem and the painting Snow over Rivers and Mountains (Figure 8.10).

Figure 8.10
After Wang Wei's Snow over Rivers and Mountains by Wang Shimin (1592–1680).

We cannot find any existing paintings by Wang Wei. Here is a painting imitating his style hundreds of years later.

The connection between poetry and music or painting leads us to a conclusion that poetry is an art that harmonizes both musicality of word pronunciation and images of word meanings. In another word, poetry adopts forms and conventions to suggest different interpretations to words, or to stimulate emotive responses from the musicality in the sound of words and images in the description. Rhetorical devices such as assonance, alliteration, onomatopoeia and rhythm are used to achieve musical effects. The use of ambiguity, symbolism, and irony allows a poem open to multiple explanations. Simile, metaphor, and metonymy create a resonance between images—a layering of meanings, forming connections to ideas previously not perceived.

The "soul" of poetry

The musicality and space of imagination enable poetry to convey people's emotions and ideals. Since the beginning of poetry, it has become a way for people to express their feelings, especially, when their hearts overflow with immense joy or sorrow. Here is a poem by Alfred, Lord Tennyson (Figure 8.11).

Figure 8.11
Alfred, Lord Tennyson (1809–1892)

Tennyson was Poet Laureate of Great Britain and Ireland during Queen Victoria's reign and remains one of the most popular British poets.

Break, Break, Break

By Alfred, Lord Tennyson

Break, break, break,
On thy cold gray stones, O Sea!
And I would that my tongue could utter
The thoughts that arise in me.

O, well for the fisherman's boy,
That he shouts with his sister at play!
O, well for the sailor lad,
That he sings in his boat on the bay!

And the stately ships go on
To their haven under the hill;
But O for the touch of a vanished hand,
And the sound of a voice that is still!

Break, break, break,
At the foot of thy crags, O Sea!
But the tender grace of a day that is dead
Will never come back to me.

Tennyson wrote the poem after the death of his friend Arthur Hallam. The poem conveys Tennyson's feelings of melancholy and nostalgia. The loss of a close friend was described in the poem as a loss throughout the world, as the poet saw the playing of young people and heard the song of the young sailor; all the things before his eyes reminded him of his friend and the irreversible loss of good times.

In ancient China, people considered that poetry came from their great zest for expressing their ambition. In the preface of *Shi Jing*, it explained the origin of poetry by the writing of the Chinese character *Shi* (meaning poetry). The ambition in our heart, when spoken, became poetry.

> 诗者，志之所致也。在心为志，发言为诗。
>
> ——《诗大序》

Confucius commented on the use of poems in *Shi Jing* in social life:

> 《诗》可以兴，可以观，可以群，可以怨；迩之事父，远之事君；多识于鸟兽草木之名。
>
> ——孔子《论语》

To Confucius, people can use poetry to express their ideas, to educate themselves, and to maintain social conventions. We probably can take a poem from *Shi Jing* as examples to explain the educational and social functions of poetry.

> **关雎**
>
> 关关雎鸠，在河之洲。窈窕淑女，君子好逑。
> 参差荇菜，左右流之。窈窕淑女，寤寐求之。
> 求之不得，寤寐思服。悠哉悠哉，辗转反侧。
> 参差荇菜，左右采之。窈窕淑女，琴瑟友之。
> 参差荇菜，左右芼之。窈窕淑女，钟鼓乐之。

The poem *Guan Ju* describes a gentleman's admiration for a lady. However, we find in the poem names and characteristics of a water bird[1] and an edible plant.[2] More importantly, the poem not only described it as normal that a gentleman was caught in love on a sleepless pillow, but also illustrated a "gentlemanlike" way to win the heart of the lady, i.e., by his cultivated talents.[3] The love between them was presented as natural and pure and can be taken

---

1. 关关雎鸠，在河之洲。
2. 参差荇菜，左右采之。
3. 琴瑟友之，钟鼓乐之。

as a good model for the young readers.

Figure 8.12
The song *Guan Ju* of *the Classic of Poetry*

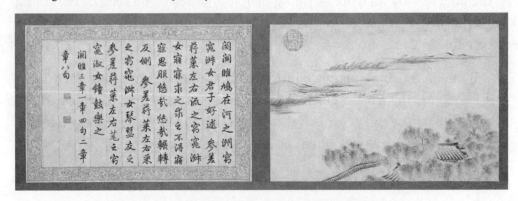

Handwritten by Emperor Qianlong in the Qing Dynasty, with accompanying painting.

In both China and the West, many poems explain moral teachings in some simple, concrete, and interesting metaphors or synecdoche. Those abstract and boring teachings can be easily remembered this way, along with the beautiful poems. We are quite familiar with the Chinese poem *Chang Ge Xing* in the Han Dynasty for encouraging young people to seize the day and work hard.

长歌行

青青园中葵，朝露待日晞。
阳春布德泽，万物生光辉。
常恐秋节至，焜黄华叶衰。
百川东到海，何时复西归？
少壮不努力，老大徒伤悲。

The poem takes the growth of sunflowers as an example to warn readers not to be lazy and idle in youth and feel regretful when they are old. Similarly, about 2,000 years later, American poet Robert Frost (Figure 8.13) compared the transient golden time to the moment of the first leaf in spring in one of his short poems.

Nothing Gold Can Stay

By Robert Frost

Nature's first green is gold,
Her hardest hue to hold.
Her first leaf's a flower;
But only so an hour.

> Then leaf subsides to leaf,
> So Eden sank to grief,
> So dawn goes down to day.
> Nothing gold can stay.

Figure 8.13
Robert Frost (1874–1963)

Frost was one of the most popular and critically respected American poets of the twentieth century.

From the mid-18th century onwards, poetry has sometimes been more generally regarded not only as a fundamental creative act employing language, but also connected to truth and philosophy. It is no longer merely a way of entertainment. It is a way of looking into life.

The philosophical ideas were illustrated in poems, and poets took the role of a philosopher, who would see through the chaotic world the truth of the universe. In one of the poems by William Wordsworth (Figure 8.14), the poet told his readers what he understood about life.

> Poets ... are not only the authors of language and of music, of the dance, and architecture, and statuary, and painting; they are the institutors of laws, and the founders of civil society ... In short, poets are the unacknowledged legislators of the world.
>
> — Percy Bysshe Shelley, *Defence of Poetry*

> Poetry is the art of uniting pleasure with truth, by calling imagination to the help of reason.
>
> — Samuel Johnson, *Lives of the English Poets: Waller, Milton, Cowley*

> I by no means rank poetry high in the scale of intelligence—this may look like affectation—but it is my real opinion—it is the lava of the imagination, whose eruption prevents an earthquake.
>
> — Lord Byron, *Letter to Annabella Milbanke*
>
> No man was ever yet a great poet, without being at the same time a profound philosopher. For poetry is the blossom and the fragrance of all human knowledge, human thoughts, human passions, emotions, language.
>
> — Samuel Taylor Coleridge, *Biographia Literaria.*

Figure 8.14
William Wordsworth (1770–1850)

William Wordsworth was a major English Romantic poet who, with Samuel Taylor Coleridge, helped to launch the Romantic Age in English literature with the 1798 joint publication *Lyrical Ballads*.

> **My Heart Leaps Up**
>
> *By William Wordsworth*
>
> My heart leaps up when I behold
>   A rainbow in the sky:
> So was it when my life began;
> So is it now I am a man;
> So be it when I shall grow old,
>   Or let me die!
> The Child is father of the Man;
>   I could wish my days to be
> Bound each to each by natural piety.

In the poem Wordsworth described the joy in the poet's heart when he saw the beautiful rainbow. Such hearty joy may indicate the constancy of his connection to nature throughout his life. He believed it was important for the poet to keep this bond to nature and feel delighted to "*contemplate similar volitions and passions as manifested in the goings-on of the Universe*" (Wordsworth, 1800).

To sum up, in Chinese culture, poetry is regarded as an artful way to express people's ambition and convey their ideals. In Western cultures, poetry is considered as artistic creation to imitate and illustrate truth. The charm of poetry lies in people's mastering of language and understanding of life.

Activity 8-5 Do you know many Chinese metrical poems used to be sung? Do you know any modern songs that were composed with poems as lyrics? Please try to search online for these "poem" songs.

Activity 8-6 The songs nowadays are similar to the poems in the old days in some ways. Can you find two Chinese and English love songs and compare them? What can you see in the comparison? Can you interpret the findings by what you know about the cultures?

8.4 Active Experimentation

The era of poetry is long gone, but it never leaves us. Though poets are still working hard writing new poems, poetry has taken back its original sound form of music and rhythm and entertaining functions. In 2016, the Swedish Academy confirmed the link between poetry and pop songs by awarding Bob Dylan the 2016 Nobel Prize in Literature "for having created new poetic expressions within the great American song tradition". That was the first time in history that a World Prize in Literature went to a singer, more unorthodox than what Bob Dylan himself would do. Dylan remained silent for some time after he heard the news. He finally agreed to accept the prize, but declined to attend the Prize banquet. He only agreed to share a recorded speech later.

> The 76-year-old singer/songwriter (Bob Dylan) began his speech by addressing a question many critics had when he first won the prize: Why was the famed literary award presented to an artist mainly seen as a musician?

"When I received the Nobel Prize in Literature, I got to wondering how exactly my songs related to literature," he said.

Using the same vivid language and circuitous storytelling that are hallmarks of his songbook, Dylan described how the classics he read in school influenced his music. "When I started writing my own songs, folk lingo was the only vocabulary that I knew, and I used it," he said. "But I had something else as well. I had principles and sensibilities and an informed view of the world, and I'd had that for a while. I learned it all in grammar school: *Don Quixote, Ivanhoe, Robinson Crusoe, Gulliver's Travels, A Tale of Two Cities*, all the rest."

"Typical grammar school reading that gave you a way of looking at life, an understanding of human nature, and a standard to measure things by," he continued. "I took all that with me when I started composing lyrics, and the themes from those books worked their way into many of my songs, either knowingly or unintentionally."

Dylan dedicates the rest of the lecture to retelling, in fantastical detail, three works of literature that specifically inspired him: *Moby Dick, All Quiet on the Western Front* and *The Odyssey*. In his speech's final moments, he acknowledges that "songs are unlike literature, they're meant to be sung, not read," before sharing a telling quote from *The Odyssey*: "Sing in me, Muse, and through me tell the story."

(Source: Maeve Mcdermott | USA Today)

Activity 7-7   Even though Bob Dylan acknowledged the influence of literature on his song writing, it seems that he does not (fully) agree with the categorization of songs into poetry or literature. What do songs and poems have in common? Do you think he deserves that literature award or such an award was a mistake? Discuss it with your friends, and support your argument by what you know about poetry.

Activity 7-8   Believe it or not, modern poems can often be rapped because they have rhythms and rhymes. Do you want to have a try? Here are some tips.

1. Pick a topic. Rappers used their lyrical expression to become advocates for change in their communities by using their words as weapons. When you choose a poem, think about the topic you

would like to develop. Think of what inspires you, e.g., things in life that touch you deeply, the most recent frustration, and try to write from there. The poem you have chosen can be used in any part to enhance the power of your song. Don't hold yourself back! You can explore new ways of building rhyme. You can even try taking on a different persona.

2. Sit down and write. When writing your first rap, give yourself certain rules that take the ego out of the process. Free styling is also a fun exercise that we recommend trying (you'd be surprised at how poetic you are when you speak from a place of spontaneity!). Make sure that you pay attention to any patterns in your typical rhyme scheme and try to switch it up.

3. Rehearse your rap. Rap is an oratory art; it isn't written to be read as much as it is written to be heard. After you've finished your rhymes you've got to speak them with confidence. This may require a few awkward rehearsals in front of the mirror, but once you become confident and comfortable in your bars you're ready to take your words to the people (adapted from the source: https://powerpoetry.org/actions/5-tips-using-rhythm-and-rap).

8.5 Chapter Summary

Though the trends of globalization affect many aspects of cultures, including literature, poetry may be the most resistant to such trends because of its universal aesthetic characteristics (see the core items of art by Dutton (2009) in Chapter 7), which is valued by UNESCO (2009) as one of the primary sources of cultural diversity because such artistic creation spans *"the spectrum of human activity"* (*ibid*, p.167).

In this chapter we mainly compare the two different styles in Chinese and English poetry, i.e., sonnet and *Ci*. Both sonnet and *Ci* originated from folk songs, and were very popular in history. Through the stories about them, we see the interaction of poetry and culture. The two styles were chosen because poetry satisfied people's needs to express their emotions in a certain cultural background. These poetic styles evolved over time along with the mainstream culture and was promoted not only by fashion, but also by the mainstream cultural trend, such as Renaissance in the West and leisure life of literary men in China. From another perspective, these two styles also conveyed the popular thought and feelings in their cultures, just like other art forms. Sonnet spread from Italy to other European countries with the popular trend of humanism, eternal art, and *carpe diem* (meaning making the most of the present time and giving little thought to the future). *Ci* conveyed literary men's joys and sorrows in the time of peace, war and social turmoil.

The development of both styles was also contributed by poets' efforts as well. The style has often been formed by the style of the "strong poets," i.e., the most renowned poets (or the Heroes in the cultural level model of Hofstede et al.), and the "weak poets" only follow.[1] Imitation is an almost subconscious order given by the tradition, i.e., when one thinks "sonnet," for example, one thinks all the sonnets one has read, and as a result, often ends up writing a sonnet like Shakespeare, John Milton, or Elizabeth Browning (Turco, 2000), just like people often think of the familiar lyrics in the Song Dynasty when mentioning *Ci*.

Comparing the examples of the sonnets and *Ci* in the above, we might find that in two languages and poetic styles, love can be described in different ways. The sonnet seemed to be more closely constructed by the themes ("to stop thinking about you" or "comparing you to a summer") and subjects ("I" or "thou"). A topic is given at the beginning, elaborated in the second part, contradicted in the third part, and resolved in the end. From this perspective, *Ci* seemed quite loose, often started from sporadic objects seen by the poets. But these objects are the ones to trigger sentiment. So the circumstance and feelings can be unified as one. The first part of the poem is usually the pavement for the following part, where the feelings are more explicitly presented.

From the language point of view, the structure of the sonnets might be connected to the characteristic of the subject-prominent language which emphasizes the relationship between the subject, predicate, and other parts of the sentence. The coherence between sentences is also emphasized. The loose structure of *Ci* can be related to the characteristics of a topic-prominent language like Chinese. The speaker cares more about the relationship between a topic and the comment on it. The connection among sentences is quite implicit and vague.

From the cultural point of view, the structure of the sonnets seems to be in light with the traditional logic theory since ancient Greece. Truth needs to be proven by logic or facts. When an argument or question is raised at the

---

1. Words of Prof. Harold Bloom, quoted in Sun, Forward to the Chinese Version, 2004, p.2.

beginning, it must be evidenced and reasoned out in the middle, and resolved in the end. The Chinese lyrics read more like Chinese painting. The poets did not care what exactly the real things were like. In their mind, human and nature were unified. When they were sad, things were gloomy. When they were happy, things were colorful and rejoiced. We see again in poetry the distinction between rational thinking in the west and emotional thinking in China.

We can see from the comparison the interactions between poetry and culture as well. The structure of poems, e.g., meters, rhymes and rhythm, need to match the characteristics of a language, so as to be pleasant to ears and easy to be performed. At the same time, these styles often appeared along with the popular trends of thought in history. There might be adaptations and evolutions, e.g., as one style is introduced from one language to another, or developed in history. All these adaptations are for the convenience of the language users and make the old ones more "fashionable" and new. Poetry is for people's delight, describes people's ideas and expresses their emotion. Art must serve the people.

8.6 Case Study Assignment

Read the article below and answer the following questions.

> **Trends: Tourist attractions encourage visitors to recite ancient poems for free entry**
>
> *By Global Times | MAY 04, 2023*
>
> During the May Day holidays, many ancient tourist attractions nationwide encouraged visitors to recite ancient poems in exchange for free entry. This new means helped boost local tourism with the help of traditional culture. At the gate to Tengwang Pavilion in East China's Jiangxi Province, visitors could enter the scenic spot by reciting the ancient poem Preface to the Pavilion of Prince Teng. Similar activities were held in the provinces of Hunan, Sichuan, and Henan. While the activity led to some loss in ticket revenue, experts believe that these activities are not only an important manifestation of cultural inheritance, but also an important measure to promote the integration of culture and tourism.
>
> (Source: https://www.globaltimes.cn)

Questions:

(1) What do you think about tourist attractions encouraging people to recite poems for free entry?

(2) How many ancient poems about tourist attractions do you know? Which tourist attractions would you like to visit for free by reciting poems about them?

(3) In cross-cultural communication, if we would like to promote our poetry, do you have a better plan/program for it (by using the cultural product design model in Chapter 7)?

References

Cuddo, J. A. (1977). *A dictionary of literary terms.* Doubleday & Company, Inc.

Dutton, D. (2009). *The art instinct: Beauty, pleasure, and human evolution.* Bloomsbury Press.

Oppenheimer, P. (1982). *The origin of the sonnet. Comparative Literature, 34*(4): 289–304. https://doi.org/10.2307/1771151

Schein, E. (1984). Coming to a new awareness of organizational culture. *Sloan Management Review, 25*(2): 3–16.

Turco, L. (2020). *The book of forms* (5th edition). University of New Mexico Press.

UNESCO. (2009). *Investing in cultural diversity and intercultural dialogue.* UNESCO.

Wordsworth, W. (1800). *Preface to lyrical ballads.* http://www.bartleby.com/39/36.html.

Hu, S. (2003) Ci xuan xu [Preface to the collection of Chinese Ci]. In X.D.Wang & D.Yang (Ed.), *Ci qu yanjiu [Studies on Chinese Ci and Qu].* Hubei Education Press.

Lu, Y. (2024). *Wenhualou cihua [The study of poetry in Wenhualou].* Retrieved from Baidu Baike [Baidu Encyclopedia] https://baike.baidu.com/ (Original work published 1848).

Shi, Z. (2004). *Cixue mingci shiyi·da/xiao ci [Definitions of terms in the study of Ci: Da/xiao ci].* Zhonghua Book Company.

Sun, K. Y. (2004). *Ci yu wenlei ya jiu [Studies on Ci and genre].* Peking University Press.

Xia, C. T., & Zhang, Z. (2005) *Jin yuan ming qing ci xuan [Collections of Ci in Jin, Yuan, Ming and Qing dynasties].* Renmin Literature Publishing House.

Xie, W. L. (1959). *Cixue zhinan [Guide to Ci studies].* Zhonghua Book Company.

Xie, T. F. (1999). *Songci bian [Analysis of Song Ci].* Shangha Guji Press.

Yuan, X. P. (1999). *Zhongguo wen xue shi [History of Chinese Literature]* (Vol. 3). Higher Education Press.

作者简介

田美 西安交通大学外国语学院教授、博士生导师、国际教育学院副院长,英国巴斯大学博士。曾赴英国伦敦大学教育学院进行学术交流。主持国家自然科学基金、教育部人文社科基金等科研课题 13 项、陕西省高等教育教学改革等教改课题 8 项。主编英文专著(专刊)4 部,发表论文 50 余篇。中国高等教育学会学习科学分会常务理事、中国教育发展战略学会国际教育专委会常务理事。曾获陕西省高等学校人文社会科学研究优秀成果奖三等奖、西安交通大学教学成果特等奖(3/10)。研究兴趣包括留学生学情调查、跨文化适应与认同、质化研究方法等。

彭凤玲 西安交通大学外国语学院教授、硕士生导师、博士,美国科罗拉多大学博尔德分校访问学者。出版专著 2 部,译著 1 部,发表论文 10 余篇,参编教材 10 部。曾获 2021 年外研社"教学之星"大赛全国一等奖、2020 年全国高校教师教学创新大赛(第六届外语微课大赛)三等奖(省部级)。研究方向为区域国别研究。

杨瑞英 西安交通大学外国语学院教授、博士生导师,新加坡国立大学博士。曾赴美国密歇根大学、荷兰格罗宁根大学进行学术交流。主持国家社科基金、教育部人文社科基金等多项研究课题,发表 SSCI 及 CSSCI 论文多篇,出版专著 2 部,主编、参编英语教材 15 部。研究兴趣包括语篇体裁分析、学术英语教学、语料库语言学等。

Carla BRIFFETT AKTAS 西安交通大学外国语学院副教授,英国兰卡斯特大学博士。主持西安交通大学、香港教育大学和香港市政府资助科研课题。在 *Teaching in Higher Education*、*Children & Society* 等国际期刊发表论文多篇。美国教育研究协会（AERA）、英国教育研究协会（BERA）、国际比较教育学会（CIES）会员。研究兴趣包括学生声音、教学法和社会公正教育。

陈大地 荷兰威登堡大学商学院副院长、副教授、硕士生导师，阿姆斯特丹大学语言中心首席讲师、英国高等教育学会会士（FHEA）。博士毕业于荷兰莱顿大学教育研究院，曾担任教师培训师和国际学术期刊评审，参与并完成多项国际合作研究项目。教授跨文化管理、学术研究方法以及教育管理硕士专业课程。研究方向为外语教师跨文化认同、跨文化交际能力培养、国际高等教育管理等。

韩璐 东北师范大学美术学院雕塑系副教授、硕士生导师、艺术学博士。中国美术家协会会员、中国雕塑学会会员、中国工艺美术学会、雕塑专业委员会会员、吉林省美术家协会雕塑艺术委员会副主任、长春市青年美术家协会理事。作品多次入选国家级展览并获奖，并被国内外多家美术馆、艺术机构、高校收藏。研究方向为美术理论与创作研究。

葛冬梅 西安交通大学外国语学院副教授，自1996年以来从事大学英语、英语写作、学术英语、中西文化比较等课程的教学。曾获陕西高等学校人文社会科学研究优秀成果三等奖，外研社"教学之星"大赛全国复赛特等奖、全国决赛三等奖，西安交通大学授课竞赛一等奖。